How Things Work
(or not really do)
An attempt to understand how our minds shape communication in organisations

First Edition

How Things Work
(or not really do)

An attempt to understand how our minds shape communication in organisations

First Edition
Self-Published by Ulrich Kies

HOW THINGS WORK
(OR NOT REALLY DO)

AN ATTEMPT TO UNDERSTAND HOW OUR MINDS SHAPE COMMUNICATION IN ORGANISATIONS

ULRICH KIES

2020, 1st Edition, corrections included Nov. 1st, 2020

ISBN 9798690624712

Edited by: *me*
Cover design: *Paper 53, GIMP, my iPad and myself*
Image sources: *Paper 53, GIMP and myself*
Fonts on Cover and in Illustrations: *Neil* by
ZETAfonts in Johannesburg, South Africa and *Bebas
Neue* (font family) by Dharma Type

Ebook template: *Book Template for Amazon KDP and
Google Play* https://tinyurl.com/ltxtemplate by
Clemens Lode at lode.de

Dedication

To all of You that have inspired my thoughts and ideas
!!

 Ulrich

Contents

Preface

This book is not a scientific analysis and discussion, nor is it attempting to provide solutions that can readily be implemented in any kind of organisational setting. It is also not a playbook or else for managers and others seeking a recipe on how to change their organisation into a more effective one. This book is my attempt to describe and explain what I am experiencing and observing in my work and private life, from stories told by friends and also me reading and watching the news. I tried to unveil recurring patterns, the mechanics behind them and finally ventured to assemble the bits and pieces into a framework that could help to explain those experiences and observations. Improving our understanding of how organisations work is essential. Organisations are everywhere: companies, politics, public administrations, and many others. We witness epic failures of organisations, experience mysterious ways of their workings and are often wondering how specific organisations survive the way they are - yet, they do. Does it have to be like this? Can a given organisation be, e.g. 10x as effective as it currently is?

If you are interested in understanding a bit more about how organisations work and why they work the way they do, this book might provide you with some useful thoughts and concepts. The solutions that I describe are my conclusions from applying the framework assembled before. You may find some pleasing, others rather obvious and others that I would have forgotten or not thought of.

Ulrich Kies
Ingelheim, Germany, August 2020

Abstract – TL;DR*

Organisations revolve all-around information. How they take up information from the surrounding world and turn it into decisions and then actions to influence the world is critical to their success – i.e. how well it serves their underlying purpose – making money or making the world a better place. Organisations consist of people, and people have brains that have limitations when it comes to processing information (aka to listen, think, and speak). The available bandwidth is severely limited, all information is processed against how the brain believes the world looks like and not against reality, and on top of that, there are misunderstandings, stereotypes, noises, and even different languages and cultures, let alone different people. Yet, we typically do not act alone but come together to work as groups, teams or organisations to combine and fortify our individual capabilities and limitations. Structuring an organisation in a way that lets information flow most efficiently and reducing as far as possible whatever gets lost when people connect to each other will make the organisation act more productively and much faster. Also, make sure that people have the same understanding of what is written or said – spend a good portion of efforts into building up and aligning your teams world model. Technology might help by providing communication tools, provide information directly to the ones that need it, and perform some pre-screening and pre-structuring to fight the information flood.

*too long; didn't read

Introduction

Interacting with other people is an integral part of our daily life. We live in families, go to work in some company or workshop, are members of parties or sports clubs or follow our faith in religious communities. Nothing around us is possible or thinkable without interaction with others – even eating, drinking, sleeping etc. are all only possible thanks to others collaborating with us up close or at a far distance. There is strong evidence that our brain developed when we started to interact with each other as hunters-gatherers about 2 million years ago [24]. Likely, it was the brain developing in size and capabilities that allowed us to live in communities, to split our activities to keep us alive among the members of the community, make plans for the future and learn from the past. Much of this requires sharing of thoughts, feelings and ideas to pool the individuals brains into a much larger and much more capable group brain. [63] The size of the brain seems to have a direct relation to the size of communities we are able to live in, indicating that it takes a tremendous cerebral activity to be a part of a group, to know and keep track of each member, to organise and communicate with the members. These groups of hunter-gatherers were so to speak the primordial organisation, the predecessor of our companies, clubs, governments etc. at the time when the brain's capacities and the capabilities of social interaction of groups of humans co-evolved. (in fact – we must assume that this co-evolution continues, albeit not at a speed that is observable over the brief streak of time since we started thinking about brains). The way we humans are, how we maintain our life, is only thinkable within some form of an organisation If our brain and organisational activities are so closely linked, why do we, during countless coffee breaks, at the water-cooler or when meeting friends in the evening, almost always discuss how things are not working in our company, community etc. as they should. Why do we feel that it all could be more productive, faster, more consistent?

- Do we really understand how organisations work?

- Why do organisations work as they do?

- Do we know what we need to do to really improve the way things are working?

- How does optimal communication look like?

- Is there a limit to what is achievable, like the maximum height of a tree or the speed at which living beings can move?

- Which element's properties define such limit?

- How does a perfect organisation look like (effective, flexible, resilient and innovative? – how much of it?)?

To come closer to answering these questions, I will look into the bits and pieces that make up an organisation, at how they function and how they are assembled to the overall structure. We will examine how information flows through an organisation at its "atomic" level – the individuals that make up an organisation – and at large scale, and try to understand how communication works and where we encounter limits and pitfalls. After all, for most of us working in companies, administrations, offices, clubs etc. communication, transforming information, sending out information is what we call work. And we almost always do this as a member of some organisation. We will see that it is nearly impossible to think up an organisation without communication. Communication is the essential ingredient that makes up an organisation. If you take away the communication from an organisation, the organisation itself is gone, too. On the following pages, I will try to explore how communication works in organisations, what the most important components are, which abilities and limitations they have, and how the interaction works – or doesn't work in the end. In the scope of such exploration is all the information flow within an organisation and across its boundaries, no matter which channel the information flows through. As the information flows through an organisation, taking up information, thinking about it, and sending out the result of such thinking go hand in hand. I will include the thinking part whenever I speak of communication or communicating. There is no communication without thinking (though sometimes people seem to be able to leave out that part of the process easily). I will not venture deeply into the realms of psychology, emotions, feelings and the role they play in communication. It is a truly important factor; however, it is a research field of its own and would go far beyond

the possibilities of this book. I will make reference
though here and there. Other than that my description will keep a rather technical view and language
and try to include the psychological part in the con-
solidated view.

Basic elements and concepts

Let me first provide a brief overview of the basic elements and concepts used in this text before we dive into some more details. As any kind of explanation of the elements and concepts will be somehow circular with each explanation of one element or concept requiring the notion of many elements, I should start with stating that a network consists of nodes and edges and that communication is the exchange of information and then move bottom-up from the more basic elements to the more elaborate concepts.

3.1 Information

Communication being the exchange of information between nodes (people, computers, etc.) makes information a significant object of our considerations. Commonly, knowledge, data, and information are used with a similar meaning; however, they are not the same, but still interrelated. Therefore, it is essential that we describe the differences between these three terms and the relation between them. A prominent way of doing so is the DIKW pyramid or hierarchy, adding wisdom as the fourth category [1]. Bottom-up, the hierarchy follows an increasing amount of context and understanding. Data, not having any context, become information by being put into context (24 °C →24 °C melting point of coconut oil). Information becoming knowledge by adding answers to *'how (to melt coconut oil)'* and finally wisdom explaining the why (I need liquid coconut oil to prepare my exotic salad dressing).   Roughly speaking,

when it comes to communication, data and information are what is being transmitted, while knowledge and wisdom are only existing in an individual's brain [40]. Knowledge is not really stored, in the original sense of the meaning, within the neurons of the brain, rather, the networks of neurons, their structure and their state is knowledge. As we will see later, this is becoming important when we look at how information is processed, and collaboration is happening within an organisation. From a theoretical perspective, information is also associated with newness (See also section 4.1). The first time I receive a message, this message contains information, the second and

third time, that same message is not really contain-
ing any additional information (other than that the
one I am talking to tends to forget what he or she
told just a few minutes before). Information can be
of different qualities, it can be very accurate or less
accurate, it can be complete or incomplete, it can be
consistent or not, it can be concise or expansive and
repetitious. Above all, it is often changing over time,
i.e. it is dynamic. Furthermore, information can be in
existence but not available, be it that the one needing
it doesn't have it or that it cannot be found among an
abundance of other information. The latter is a more
and more central issue of the information age.

3.2 Process model

One of the fundamental activities in communication
is the processing of information. In the communication model, as we will see later, such information
processing includes encoding and decoding as fundamental types of such processing steps. In a more general view (borrowing from the general process model
in engineering), processing can be described as the
transformation of matter, energy, and information
into a different set of matter, energy, and information.
When looking at communication only, we can omit
matter and – pragmatically – also energy and just
focus on the information being fed into the process,
transformed and emitted again in a different manifestation. Typically, any unit that processes informa-

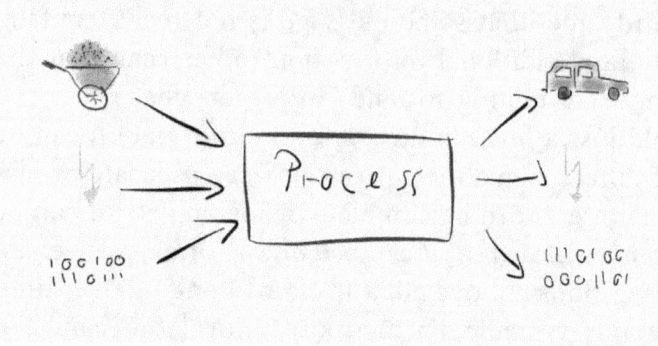

tion does so by making use of information that is already available (such as experience, rules, knowledge,
...) and keeps part of the incoming information to increase and optimise knowledge, rules, etc. technically
speaking – information is stored Additionally, incoming and outgoing information will be subjected to pre-
and post-processing to make information usable and
understandable and only use what is needed – which
represents filters/processors of various kinds. Finally,
a unit that is processing information will typically be
able to take up information from various senders and
also be able to send out to different recipients.

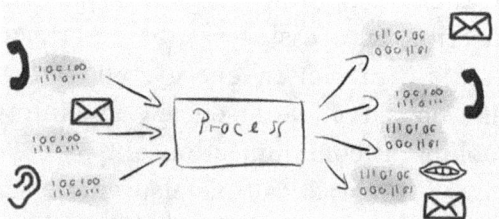

3.3 Node

The location of information processing, the place where all this happens is called 'Node'. A node is one of the fundamental elements of a network, representing a unit that is connected to other similar units through connections or edges. It typically capable of receiving, processing, and emitting information, following the process model discussed above. As a node receives Information, the incoming information is transported to it through a given channel, decoded, and then run through several filters before it becomes available for processing. For the activity of processing, the information is partially stored and transformed together with information that is retrieved from the node's storage. The result is then run through the outbound filters and encoded ready to be transmitted.   On a human level, a person receives

acoustic, sensory, or visual information, decodes, i.e. hears, sees, feels, or reads and then tries to make sense of the received information. Finally, that processed information will be sent out by speaking, writing, physical means, body language so the other members of the organisation or the outside environment can work with that information. However, in all these process steps, noise and filters have a strong influence on the outcome. Noise in the respective channel (audible noise, blurred vision, etc.) will distort the incoming information before decoding. Subsequently, in the process of decoding all the way down to making sense of the information filters are at work. Biases, cognitive faults, and fallacies will strongly influence how the information reaches the cognitive system. We will see later how the information coming through will have a positive and negative feedback effect on the filter tuning (*'filter bubble'* inside the brain). It is vital to notice that those filters mostly work unconsciously, i.e. we have to work hard to even detecting them being at work! For the outgoing information, a similar set of filters come into play, from conscious filtering such as intention, politics, delay, wilful misinformation, etc. to unconscious filters influencing how we send out the information in writing speaking or other visual signals. Computers and computer systems can be viewed either as part of a human node (to the extent that a Laptop, Phone, etc. is used to store information that is practicably inaccessible to the rest of the organisation) or as a node in itself (such as collaboration software, cloud services, ERP, etc.) connecting to its users.

3.4 Edges

In a network, the edges, better known as connections, essentially are describing how nodes interact with each other. Those connections can either have a direction (Person A speaks to Person B) or without direction, thus indicating a more general communication between two nodes (a dialogue, a discussion). These connections also represent the communication channels that are used (spoken words, writing, etc.) and the mode of the communication (e.g. asynchronous – email, does not need to be read once it lands in your mailbox; synchronous – meeting, you cannot attend a meeting a week after it took place). The connections also have a capacity specific to the channel that is used – in a conversation, the limit is the speed at which people can talk and listen. If e.g. automated email is used, one can dump an almost unlimited amount of information onto the receiver within seconds. However, under normal circumstances, email speed is just writing/reading speed. Computer systems, as nodes, can communicate with almost unlimited bandwidth, it just depends on how much we are willing to invest. However, at the very moment that electronic communication arrives at a human node, speed goes down to the human level.

3.5 Communication

Communication is typically defined as the exchange of information between nodes of a communication network (between people, systems, etc.) The general process involves a sender wishing to send information to a receiver. To do so, the information has to be encoded into a signal so it can be sent through the chosen communication channel. The receiver, in turn, needs to decode the signal into the message. Typically, any chosen channel is influenced by a given amount of noise that distorts the signal on its way to the receiver and in turn can render the received information being different from the one that has been sent. Or – from a more human-centred perspective:

In an organisational context, the channels most often used are speech and writing. The former mostly being in-person communication, telephone or other remote voice connection. In the time domain, the communication can be immediate or open-ended if, e.g. voice messages are sent that can be listened to at any time. Often human communication occurs in more than one mode at a time. E.g. speech can be accompanied by visual signals (in person, video telephony) adding a channel for additional (meta) information. Writing is mostly employed in email, chats, letters, minutes, presentations, and documents being sent around. Communication can either occur as a dialogue (1:1), broadcast (1: everybody) or multicast (1: selected group) – (also a many: many communication is possible, however strictly speaking peo-

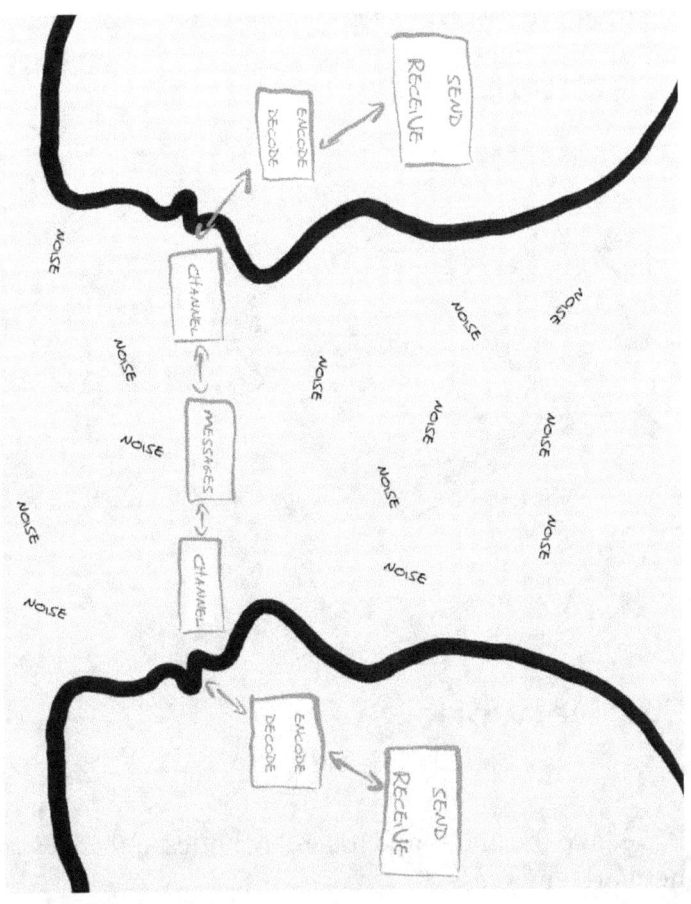

ple cannot consciously listen to more than one message at a time, any additional message would have to be regarded as noise) Furthermore, communication can be immediate, interactive, as in a dialogue or a meeting (synchronous communication) or with sending and receiving being temporally separated, as in emails, voice mails, books, documentation (asynchronous documentation)

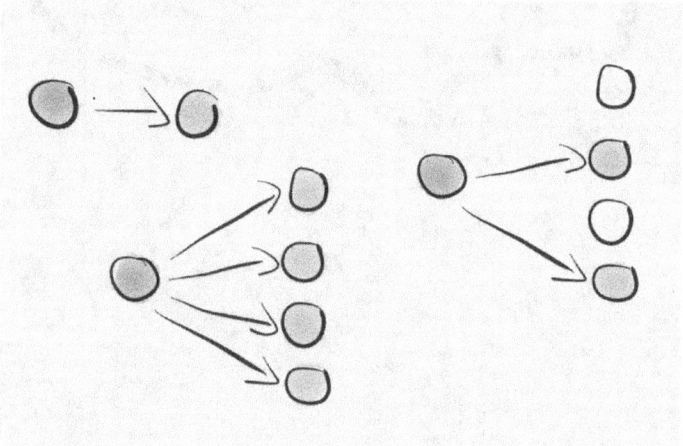

3.6 Network

If we take the above and assemble nodes and edges, a network emerges:

According to common definitions, a network consists of several similar elements that are related to each other in a specific manner: "A Network is a system that consists of many similar parts that are connected

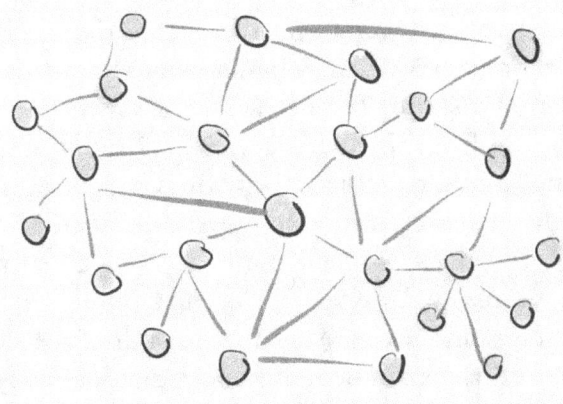

to allow movement or communication between or along the parts." [11]. In network science, a network consists of nodes and the pathways that connect these nodes, making nodes and these pathways, also called edges central elements of a network. In the context of a view on communication in an organisational environment, we speak about a network of people, communication devices, and computer systems that all interact and communicate with each other. An essential characteristic of a network is its topology, how are its parts being laid out and interrelated. Networks can be, e.g. star-like, with a central node at which all connections meet or like a tree, with connections branching off at each hierarchical level or meshed whit ordered or random connection between all nodes not following any hierarchy. Nodes, as we have seen, can have multiple connections, or just one, these connections can be strong or weak. When drawing a network of communication, we have to acknowledge that we are drawing the sum of communication interactions over a given time-frame rather than a static network. Communication networks, such as organisations evolve and change over time and typically are not static. The network of this week might be different from that of last week, 12 months view showing another picture. Networks can be formal, meaning that they are constituted and documented in a more or less official manner, such as companies have organisational charts, and public institutions have some formal structure, or informal, like a network of friends or acquaintances that just happen to be related without any formal description or documentation. Networks can be set up in an ad-hoc manner, like people meeting to complete a given task or have a static character like a company, a soccer club, etc. (understanding that in many companies' organisational charts are of ever-changing nature).

3.7 The Organisation

An organisation is a structured group of people that meet or interact to pursue collective goals. It is characterised by the relation between its members. An organisation is always a network, it can be seen as a specific form of a communication network in which, e.g. the topology, the structure of the relationships between the individual members, is typically given by an organisation chart Typically, organisations are open systems, they affect their environment and are affected by their environment likewise. With the purpose of the organisation commonly lying outside of the organisation, organisations must take up something from the environment, convert it and feed it back in such a way that it has the desired impact on the environment.

For most organisations, especially companies, that 'something' is precisely what the technical process model describes: matter, energy, and information. Money being also a form of information (aside from cash being also matter) and considering that there is no truly 'matter less' way of working, this is true also for companies that just trade and process information. Coming back to the purpose of an organisation, only what (matter, energy, information) transgresses the organisations' boundary can influence the value that an organisation can create and the effect it can have. Leaving aside tangible things and focusing on office organisations, the activities of an organisation can be reduced to: taking up information, converting, processing it, and dissipating it back to the organisational environment (that could be other organisations, individuals, etc.), in short: communication. With the modern economy largely being built on services and knowledge work, most office organisations essentially are information transforming organisations. *Why do we need organisations in the first place?* Like the primordial groups of hunters and gatherers, organisations typically are evolving to employ and organise a form of division of labour, allowing large numbers of specialists of various professions to efficiently work together. To efficiently work together, the overall tasks have to be split into portions for each member, that member has to be instructed of it and probably be provided with the required skills and then finally the whole organisation has to be orchestrated to actually perform the organisation's task to react to signals coming from the organisations outside and in return exert the desired effect onto it. In short, the incoming information has to be distributed to the ones processing it and then be assembled again so it can be put into action in the organisations' outside environment.

Information Theory

In the previous sections, we have seen all the main building blocks of organisations, networks and communication. However, before we can understand how it all works together and before making any inferences, on the whole, as well as the boundary conditions that apply and the limitations that exist, we must take a more in-depth look into some of the related theory. Taking a glimpse into the realms of information theory. The whole topic is by far too large to provide a comprehensive overview; however, I believe that understanding some of the concepts around information and its transmission will help to understand the subsequent paragraphs in a much more complete way. If this should be too much theory for you at the moment, just skip it, it will stay, so you always can go back.

4.1 Shannon and Weaver's model

Typically, the workings of communication are described by various communication models, one of the classic, technical ones having been developed by Claude Shannon [61][62]. The basic elements of communication he defined as:

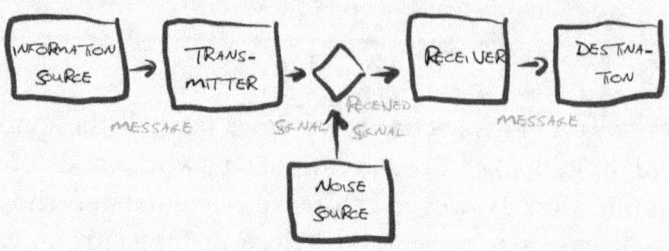

- An Information Source which is the person or system or thing producing a message (the idea or content that he or she wishes to send)

- A Transmitter (or encoder) being needed to convert the message into a form that can be transmitted through the selected channel.

- A Channel being the medium or infrastructure that is used to send the message from the Transmitter to the Receiver, e.g. electrical wires, plain air, etc.

- A Receiver doing just the opposite from the Transmitter, it converts the received signal into the message

- A Destination being the person or system for whom or which the original message was intended.

- Noise, distorting the signal while being sent and this rendering the conversion process at the Receiver's end faulty. Noise can be external, e.g. sound inhibiting a person from hearing correctly what was being said or internally, e.g. mistakes in the encoding or decoding process

Further, Shannon and Weaver introduced the concept of information entropy to quantify the amount of information contained in a message. In a nutshell: the amount of information that can be found in a particular message depends on the context that this message is being sent within – it relates to the probability of a message. The lower the probability is that a certain message is being sent, the higher is the amount of information contained therein. Entropy, according to Shannon, is simply the *"amount of information"* contained in a message:

$$H = - \sum_i p_i \log_2 p_i$$

Where p_i is the probability of character/ letter, *i* appearing in the sequence of characters in the message. Applying this to the 26-letter alphabet, each letter has the same probability of appearing in a given text – at first sight though – in reality, letters such as 'E' have a higher probability of appearing in, German texts for example than the letter 'X'. (Symbols outside of the context of an alphabet have no information content at all within that respective context.) Another aspect to note is that the density of information can vary, i.e. the amount of information contained within a specific sequence of symbols, syllables, etc. High redundancy of information within a message will decrease its information density. Also, the language used might have an influence, English, for instance, was measured to have an information rate that is 20% higher than the information rate of German – using average normal speaking speed. [56] The dependence

of information content on the context also has important implications when it comes to communication
bandwidth: the more common knowledge two parties of a communication share, the less information is
needed to submit a given message. 'Car' just uses 3
letters to describe a sophisticated and complex thing
without needing to explain every bit and piece. This
is also the idea behind language, culture, etc.: power-
ful concepts and ideas that can be described with little
information. It is working perfectly, if both parties of
a communication activity share the same upfront information, e.g. by speaking the same language, coming from a similar cultural background, etc. – if not,
it lays a foundation for beautiful misunderstandings.
Looking at the quality of the communication process,
Warren Weaver described three levels that are of influence:

- *"LEVEL A. How accurately can the symbols of
  communication be transmitted? (The technical
  problem.)*

- *LEVEL B. How precisely do the transmitted symbols convey the desired meaning? (The semantic
  problem.)*

- *LEVEL C. How effectively does the received meaning affect conduct in the desired way? (The effectiveness problem.)"* [62]

The technical problem stated in LEVEL A has been
intensely discussed by Shannon and been detailed
above. LEVEL B requires us to look at the meaning
of 'Meaning' first. According to the Merriam Webster

Dictionary , meaning is:

- *"the thing one intends to convey especially by language [...]*
- *the thing that is conveyed especially by language [...]*
- *something meant or intended [...]*
- *the logical connotation of a word or phrase [...]*
- *the logical denotation or extension of a word or phrase"* [45]

While the first and third descriptions take the viewpoint of the sender of a message, i.e. what is intended to be sent, the second views the process from the end of the receiver, i.e. what is actually conveyed to him or her. Finally, the last two lines treat meaning as something objective that seems to be independent of the sender and the receiver. In the following, I will take the viewpoint that the meaning of a message can best be described by what the receiver understands when receiving a message. In this, I am following Weaver, who states for LEVEL C that the effectiveness of a communication process is described by how it affects the conduct [of the receiver] in the desired way. At a later stage, we will see how much whatever information enters the brain of an individual its interpretation will depend on the context it finds there.

We now can enhance the Shannon's communication model or better scale it up with Weaver's concept by embedding the technical sequence of LEVEL A:

message – transmitter – signal /noise – receiver –
message

into a similar sequence on LEVEL B:

meaning – transmitter – message/noise – receiver –
meaning

and finally on LEVEL C:

intent – transmitter – meaning/noise – receiver –
intent

For each level B and C, too, an encoder, a receiver, and
a transmitter can be added and also specific noise at
each level, yielding a somewhat recursive version of
the original structure: Noise is disturbing the com-

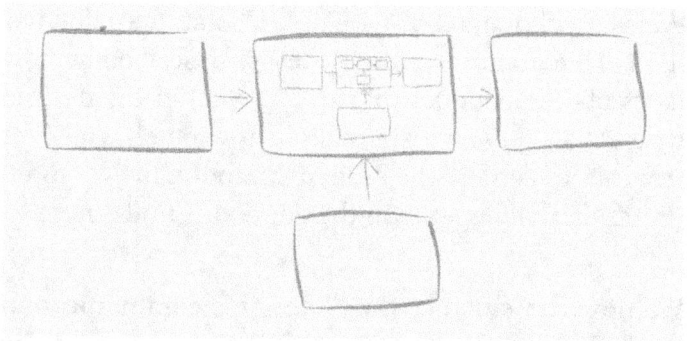

munication on all three levels, be it noise disturbing

the physical signal, be it noise changing the meaning or intents that are not understood as they were initially conceived. Such noise is an intrinsic part of human communication, so when language as the principal mode of communication has evolved, it already brought along the remedy: redundancy. All languages have a certain degree of redundancy. So, if you only partially can pick up what another person is saying, this often is enough to understand meaning and intent (body language and mimic contributing their part to meaning and intent especially). English, as an example, statistically spoken, has a redundancy of about 50%. [62], which in the end allows for easy correction and even automatic spell checking. We also can see noise here on Levels B and C. Noise can be introduced into the process at these stages, i.e. the meaning being sent over the channel is changed in the process, or some of the meaning is omitted, or some is added. So whatever gets decoded by the meaning receiver is not what has been fed to the meaning transmitter. Finally, as Weaver stated: Thirdly, It seems highly suggestive for the problem at all levels that error and confusion arise and fidelity decreases, when, no matter how good the coding, one tries to crowd too much over a channel [62]– if we overload a channel of communication – or a receiver or a transmitter – information will get lost or to be more precise it will not reach the destination

4.2 Where does unused information go?

In the sections above we saw that an essential part of the brain's function, of information processing in general, is filtering out information from the incoming and outgoing streams and not use it for the process. Where does this information go? In quantum physics information can neither be created nor can it be destroyed, as stated by the no-cloning theorem [74] and the no-deleting theorem [55]. If information is disappearing from the original system, then it can be found somewhere in the rest of the universe (no hiding theorem [59]). From a theoretical point of view, the answer to the question above is that unused information continues to exist, just somewhere else. We, our brains, usually pick up much more information than we actually need to consciously perform the given tasks, what we do not need is either filtered out or reaches our brain where it is 'stored' making it a part of our knowledge. Knowledge, as we have seen, is used when we are processing information to generate a message to communicate to others, but also to be creative, to make a decision, to reach a conclusion, etc. There is probably also a load of information in our brains that is labelled 'useless facts' that somehow made it into our brain without any purposed effort on our end.

The filtered-out part of the information either is blocked in the early stages of its processing on the way to the conscious processing, so it is "somewhere else" in the quantum physics way of thinking or depending on the position of the filtering process, or enters the unconscious part of our thinking, diffuses into the information filters, changing their tuning for the future or finds another way of entering our memory by other means, waiting to be recalled in some unexpected context at a later point in time. In an organisational environment, we see people being flooded with information, with emails, phone calls, webcasts, meetings, concepts, proposals, slides, etc. Much of that information is likely never really read or understood by the people receiving it, let alone used in any of their future work and communication. Still, it is not lost, but sitting on some email server, cloud service, or file storage and eventually gets forgotten or deleted by the annual clean-up program, the storage policy or accounts being deleted. This can turn out to be a significant problem for organisations and their . A considerable amount of cognitive capacity is used to generate and consume information and then is wasted when it cannot be put into action to generate value or purpose and likely gets forgotten with all its traces being lost (and often the information needs to be produced again). In that respect, we are close to the statement on quantum physics above – the unused information is somewhere else, just not where it is needed at the moment, and most likely it is still somewhere in the organisation's own universe.

Our brain at work

5.1 World Model

Humans, people like us, are the core part of any organisation. Therefore, understanding the limits and boundary conditions of their ability to communicate and think is key to understanding the resulting limits of communication within an organisation or a network. While the world 'happens' at an almost unlimited rate (speaking from the perspective of information theory), the rate at which we, as people, actually can participate seems to be incredibly low – which has some significant consequences We experience the world through our senses, such as hearing, seeing, feeling, etc. While the incoming signals, e.g. visual, auditory ones are typically received at a tremendous rate, that what is finally being processed consciously occurs at a much slower rate- see picture below [21]. As we can see, we receive information through our ears and eyes with an order of approximately 10 kilobit/s and close to 10 Megabit/s respectively. The level, at which we can consciously process information is many orders of magnitude lower – just 20-30 bits/s. What our mind makes of all this information is even much higher, we assume that we experience our world in Super-High-resolution 360°HD (mostly through seeing) at a rate of more than 100 Gbit /s. (we believe to see our environment in the highest possible resolution, while for the most part of our vision angle, we just sense brightness and move-

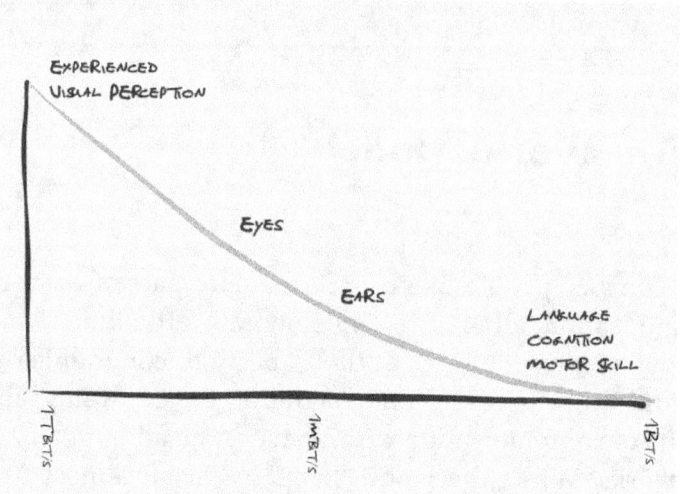

ment. The mind makes up the rest!).
Our brain has to manage the task of reducing the
flood of information we pick up down to a level of
us being able to process it consciously and then to
present us with a real-life experience that we perceive
to be happening on a much higher rate. The consequences are severe: we almost have no chance of experiencing the real world. Still, we have to base our
experience on the picture of the world that we assembled in our brain starting at the moment we were born
(or even weeks before that), it is the universe we live
in, our 'youniverse', as described by R. Epworth [20].
Consequently, almost all of our actions, our decisions
and also our perceptions are based almost exclusively
on what we believe the world to be – on our world
model. When we think, see or listen, we combine a
vast amount of information from within our brains
with a small stream of information action trickling
in from the outside to come to conclusions about the

world around us. We have models and concepts of everything around us, when we see, e.g. a cow, we do not count the number of legs, assess the shape of the body etc. and then use this evidence to consciously conclude that among all other animals we know of there must be a cow in front of us. Instead, we follow a few cues, and the brain says 'cow' based on what our internal world model tells us. We constantly model what is around us, our house, our city, our cars, etc. We have models of all the people we know within our head – that is essentially what knowing somebody is. Models of friends and our partners are more sophisticated than models of acquaintances or than models of someone we just met. This is how we can tell friends by the way they walk, laugh or even how they react. Any deviation from our model causes dissonances between our perception and our brain's expectation, so we, e.g. quickly can tell that something is wrong when our partner reacts unexpectedly. We certainly also have a model of ourselves that guides our actions down to our bodily movements. And that is really important, how would we be able to interact with all the other parts of our world model if we were not part of it. Or – in other words: what is the use of a precise model of our bedroom without knowing where our various body parts are when we need to go to the bathroom in the dark of the night? (This is called *proprioception*). Or – in different words, *"evolution has given us an interface that hides reality and guides adaptive behaviour. Space and time as you perceive them right now are your desktop [...] evolution has shaped us with perceptual symbols that keep us alive."* [27]. Rather than limiting us, this mechanism enables us to survive in a world, which is beyond our understanding. We can work with symbols and icons instead of individual grains of sand or singular trees in a wood. (All this invented by evolution to ensure the most efficient pursuit of our one and only reason to be: propagating our genes). Living, from a cognitive perspective, could be reduced to a constant sequence of us testing our hypotheses of the world around us while we navigate through our environment – we plan an action based on what we expect to happen and then take up what our perception tells us about the feedback from the world. What falls in line with our expectations somehow reinforces our beliefs and or model, what lies outside produces cognitive dissonances and either leads to the adjustment of our model by incorporating this unexpected behaviour or leads to fear, etc.

This is probably the right moment for a disclaimer: my brain, in wording the above, did some oversimplification – we certainly do something with the high bandwidth data stream flowing into our brain while it is being reduced and compressed. The brain isn't designed like an AI application, thinking, and feeling is more than just processing an input into an output, the state is the process and vice versa. There are many junctions and branches into different parts of the brain when information is prepared to be presented to the consciousness, we have reflexes that are fired without any conscious intervention, we recognise things we know, e.g. faces, cars, etc. without consciously thinking about it. (research actually postulates that the unconscious is the normal state of mind) [47][35]. In this deliberation, I am trying to focus the discussion to the conscious processing that has been shown in experiments to be happening at an impressively low rate – as described above – because this is where most of the organisational communication happens The fact that we live in our brain rather than in the world has fundamental implications when we speak about us and as well about the other individuals we interact with. We only have access to our model of them and us living in 'our world'. Other individuals only have access to their model of the world. So, if we want to work or collaborate with another individual or a group of individuals, we must try to understand how they see the world and what model they base their thoughts and actions upon. Interestingly, this understanding or not-understanding can also be observed and measured on the level of brain activity, respectively the activity of the various regions of the brain. The brains of speaker and listeners synchronise if they are speaking of and understanding within a similar context. You actually can observe that their brainwaves start to sync and similar areas of the brain get activated. However, if the context, e.g. given by setting the scene for the story they were listening to was differing between the test subjects, no such synchronicity could be observed. You can find more details and a fascinating talk on the subject by Uri Hasson here:[26] and [2].

While context somehow prepares the ground for understanding and communicating successfully, trust is another important factor to be considered. Trust is an intrinsic part of the world model, specifically of the models we have of people, organisations etc. within it. It refers to predictable behaviour, reliability and is a primary component of relationships between individuals and groups [4]. Trust also relates strongly to what general 'concept of man' we hold, what we expect from others that we are interacting with. Do we see partners everywhere or people who want to harm us, etc.?

A model in which I do not put trust cannot be used for prediction or inference and therefore is useless (or probably is not even a model in the first place). We spend our whole life building up this model, all based upon a tiny stream of information that we can take up at any given moment. Culture (tradition, ethics) takes care that this process is somehow synchronised between the individuals of a group, nation, class, etc. so at least we can expect to understand other people that were brought up in a similar context to ours. In an organisation, everybody brings along his or her own model when they start working initially. Company culture, visions, and missions, but mostly the experience of working with others help to synchronise the models of the individuals of an organisation (not to mention standard operating procedures), so in the end, we know what to expect from our co-workers, how to collaborate and what to avoid to do or say. Whatever model of the world we have in our heads, as we will see later, it will largely influence what we experience, understand, and how we act, and how we assimilate incoming information.

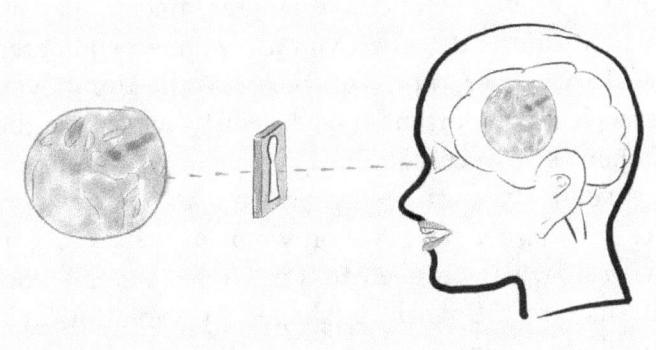

5.2 Filters and Fallacies

With our sensory organs feeding the brain with Megabits of information per second on the one hand and our conscious mind being capable of processing only tens of bits per second, on the other hand, we need to filter out roughly 99,9999% of the information that is hitting our eyes, ears, nose etc. before we can even start thinking- discarding what is not needed, while – hopefully – keeping all the important stuff. This huge reduction by many orders of magnitude shows that such filtering is a precondition to the functioning of our minds. Filters of various kinds enable us to focus on what is needed and makes living as we know it possible in the first place. On the other hand, the filters have a significant effect on how we live, and even the subtlest change in their tuning can make a big difference in where our thinking goes to and how we live. To make things worse, our understanding of the world, our world model, our perceptions and our emotions, in turn, influence how the filters are tuned. You might understand your partner differently when you are angered compared to when you are not, you only see the things you perceive as important (not the dirty dishes on the kitchen top), once you bought a yellow car yourself you suddenly start seeing yellow cars everywhere, etc. On a larger scale, we only perceive the world in terms of what we need to survive [27], our whole interface to the world is shaped by evolution in a way that we can spot ripe fruit with our eyes (colour sensing), avoid poisonous food (bitter taste and nose) and even smell which prospective partner has an immune system complementary to ours [71]. Before speaking more about the filters themselves, we will take a look at where information is processed when it reaches our mind: As mentioned above, Daniel Kahneman [32] described a fast and a slow system, System-1 and System-2.

- System-1 *"operates automatically and quickly, with little or no effort and no sense of voluntary control".*

- System-2 *"allocates attention to the effortful mental activities that demand it, including complex computations. The operations of System-2 are often associated with the subjective experience of agency, choice, and concentrations".*

System-1 is believed to be our normal state of mind, we see something and immediately have our judgement – it might be false or wrong – but at least it is available immediately. This is the system making heavy use of the filters. System-2 only runs, if we actively switch it on, as it uses quite some energy, we try to avoid using it too often. (the brain is responsible for about 20% of our total energy consumption, cognitive thinking increases that proportion even more [3]) Using it, we can override many of our filters – if we want to. The fallacies, stereotypes, biases and prejudices that System-1 brings along are curses and blessings simultaneously. We simply do not have time to consciously assemble all pixels of a sabre tooth tiger and analyse the picture before deriving a conclusion. Being a sophisticated pattern recognition engine, our brain does this unconsciously before we know it. While it might save our lives at times, or just enables us to identify the car model passing by, the brain always applies the same method, e.g. on people with blue hair or situations we believe to know (*'this never worked'*). We need to acknowledge that using stereotypes and prejudices is the normal mode of our brain at work – System-1 gets a piece of information and immediately serves an answer. We need to categorise and make pre-judgements on what we perceive, we will never have all available information in our hands to make a fully informed decision. What we can and need to work on is to keep challenging our models of the people and the world around us and make them more sophisticated step by step – use System-2 to fine-tune System-1. While we might regard the state of filters functioning as expected to be the normal state, we have to acknowledge, that even then there are some 'malfunctions' that make our thinking and perception working quite differently from what we expect. Commonly those are termed fallacies, biases, illusions, heuristics etc. I will not try to define and delineate these terms as there are no clear boundaries between them. They are all located between the sensing of our eyes and ears, etc. and the cognitive processing in our brains, trying to reduce the information flood and sometimes feeding us with an awkward selection or even wrong information. (Probably, what we nowadays see as a malfunction is just result of applying brain functions that have evolved in the early days of mankind to a world that they never have been 'designed' for.) The number of different fallacies, biases and effects that are described in today's literature seems to be un-countable with new ones still popping up now and then. An excellent place to start is the blog of Buster Benson who ventured to crawl Wikipedia for all fal-lacies and biases being listed and categorise them in a meaningful way. He came up with 4 categories that all 200+ entries he found could be sorted into [10]:

- Too much information

- Not enough meaning

- Not enough time and resources

- Not enough memory

This nicely summarises the challenges that our brain faces to match the information flood from an indefi-nitely complex environment with our limited cogni-tive resources so we can survive and proliferate. Below I list some prominent ones here that also have particular relevancy to communication in organisations (Alphabetical order):

- *Anchoring Bias* – the first bits of information we receive within a decision process or just before it is often used as an anchor point that we measure all the following against it, this works even on a subliminal level. The last number we see or hear before judging about the price of a given item influences whether we perceive it as being cheap or expensive

- *Availability Bias* – we judge based on information that is readily available rather than reasoning. E.g. if many of our friends own a red car, we tend to overestimate the ratio of red cars on the streets

- *Confirmation Bias* – we focus on information confirming our current beliefs and filter out much of what would contradict

- *Expectation Bias* – our expectation of the outcome of a certain activity influences what we actually perceive, e.g. we hear the words we expect and not the ones being said.

- *Framing Effect* – decisions are influenced by the way the choices and information are presented – we rather choose '95% fat-free' over '5% fat.'

- *Hindsight Bias* – the 'I knew it' fallacy – if we follow down a tree starting at a leaf we certainly reach the stem, our mind assumes a similar logic the other way around

- *Illusion of Understanding* – we believe we understand everyday items much better than we actually do (can you correctly sketch a bicycle without seeing one?) because we know others who can or feel that the information is only one click away

- *Narrative Fallacy* – we try to fit the information we receive into a story or a logical sequence and rather make up facts than admit that there is no story or logic

- *Social Proof Bias* – being the only one claiming a particular fact, when all others claim the opposite is extremely difficult, we often rather agree with something that seems to be wrong.

- *Sunk Cost Fallacy* – as we are all sharing a strong loss aversion, we often decide "to invest additional resources into a losing account" [32] to avoid having to admit that we were, e.g. wasting time, money, emotional efforts etc.

Many more fallacies have been described, e.g. by Daniel Kahneman [32], Nassim Nicolas Taleb [64], Steven Sloman [63], and others. Rolf Dobelly provides an almost comprehensive summary and a vast list of references in his book 'The Art of Thinking Clearly' [17] or even more complete the cognitive bias codex by Buster Benson, mentioned above [10].

To understand how those effects work, we could imagine our perception of the world to be like peeking through a keyhole to see the world, we just see a tiny bit of what is out there. Our filters, fallacies, and biases are changing what we perceive by manipulating the shape, size, and position of the keyhole. They can make us see certain things and can prevent us from perceiving others. We only see a part of the world, our filters control what we see, they sit at the door of our perceptions, and we need to invest hard cognitive work to ensure we see what we want and need to see.

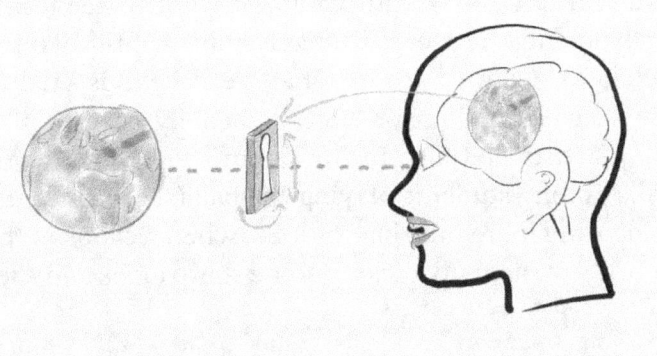

5.2.1 Example 1: our vision system

To give an example about how all this plays out, let us have a look at one of our probably most frequently used sense: seeing While seeing feels like the most natural way of acting in the world – we see what is – the reality is much more complex. Our eyes are not HD or UHD/4k 3D cameras. Instead, the eyes are built in a way that lets us see with a high resolution in colour within an angle of 2degrees only, corresponding to an area of the retina, the fovea, where most of the colour-sensitive come type vision cells are located, which is about what is covered by our thumbnail if we stretch out our arm. Beyond that, we see brightness mainly, and at the blind spot, we see almost nothing. We partially compensate for that restriction, by moving our eyes to quickly move around in so-called saccades covering different spots of interest, which is by far not touching all that is there. To some extent, we willfully focus onto what we want to see, other movements are steered unconsciously. Still, we see what we want to see or what we believe is vital to be seen. This filter or effect is heavily used by illusion artists and also in the famous video of the gorilla among students playing the ball (see [12] for the video and more information). So, when we look at the world, we actually pick up some sharp areas and a lot

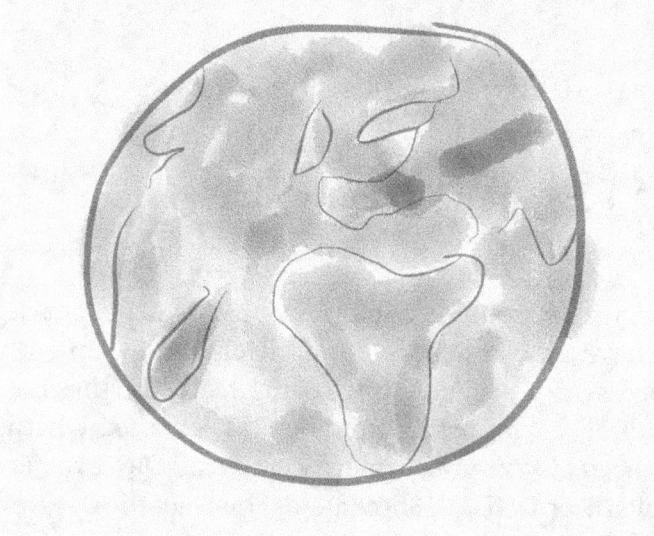

of blur fading into grey-scales in the more peripheral parts our vision as peripheral vision is dominated by

the rod cells that show luminance rather than colour
Nevertheless, our brain starts extracting and recon-

structing colours and shapes, like a circle or a sphere
and contours of yellow, brown and green embedded
in blue, replacing much of the corresponding information with concepts of lines shapes and colours –
the original information get lost mostly, most of us
won't be able to tell many details, such as the number of lines or the exact position of the colour blobs.
We simply cannot consciously work with every single
signal from one of our vision cells, we need to heavily
reduce, consolidate and conceptualise. We recognise
that something round and coloured like this and contours like that must be the earth that we have seen
so often depicted on photographs, world maps and
globes. So, our brain concludes, that we are seeing
the earth in front of us, pulls up the concept 'earth'
and starts to fill in the gaps, the blurred areas, with

our idea of that world that we have seen so often. The brain, being a pattern recognition machine, tries to find patterns, known shapes, things in whatever is presented. While my sketch clearly is not a picture of our earth, we immediately recognise it as such, even turning it into a sphere. We visually perceive the world around us in three dimensions, that is what our vision system is used to. Consequently, it tries to find some real-world meaning and adds a third dimension. However, if we compare that picture with what

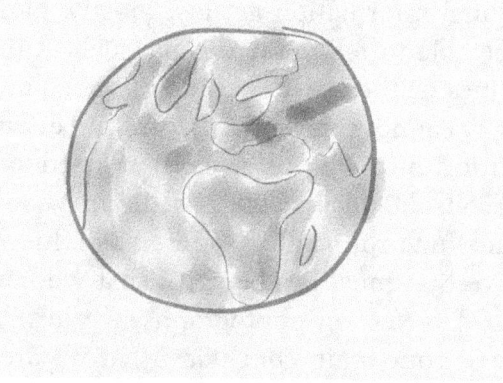

has been presented to us, we see that two blobs were

missing, one that we usually call Greenland and one known as Madagascar. Our brain didn't care, though. It had enough information to come to a conclusion, a wrong one though. This is probably the effect that is at play when New Zealand is missing from world maps all across the board [50]

5.2.2 Example 2: Colour as a concept

If you ever have tried to discuss colours such as pink, black or violet with your husband, spouse or friends, you probably started to assume that colours are concepts rather than immutable facts, culture and language influence or even determine what we perceive as colours. There are even cultures that do not have a word for what we call blue [16]. Our eyes only pick up three different colour ranges with peaks at 440nm, 545nm and 565nm corresponding to our blue, green and red sensing cone cells in our eyes respectively [33] – the rest – all Tanager Turquoise, Bossa Nova Red or Pale Peach types of colours happens in our brain or in the brains of some talented marketing people and home improvement companies or Haute couture labels.

5.3 Switching time and multitasking

The rate of 20 – 30 bit/second mentioned above describes a state in which the cognitive processes run in a more or less steady-state (flow) – staying on one line of thinking, not being disturbed putting all available capacities into action. However, this is not the natural state that we are typically in. During most of our waking time, there are many different people, activities or things that demand our attention. In each of these cases, our brain needs to decide what or whom we shall focus our attention on. While the previously described effects are more related to the act of information uptake, processing, and dissemination, determining what we perceive and how we perceive other effects relates to the way, the brain organises all this: multitasking and task switching. Each time the brain is tasked to switch from one line of activity to another, like switching from reading a book to answering a phone call or generally moving from one topic to another it has to do this actively. Contrary to popular belief, there is no real multitasking when it comes to cognitive activity. While we can, e.g. walk, talk, and breathe simultaneously, only talking usually involves cognitive processes. Adding another task, such as reading a map requires our mind to switch back and forth between talking and processing the information from the map. Our attentional filter decides what our attention is pointed at. From an evolutionary point of view, this is very important, it forces our attention to the growling sound behind us no matter if we were planning to pick up some fruit or hunt some deer. Our ears just picked up the growl of a Lion, presents it to the attentional filter, which immediately decides to forget about the deer and focuses on avoiding to be eaten. It is challenging to override the decisions of our attentional filter, a fact which social media companies use heavily by employing armies of engineers, psychologists and other scientists to extract as much attention from us as possible. [49] No matter how hard we try, we only can perform cognitive tasks sequentially. Looking deeper into how it works and what effects it has on us, we have to distinguish two timescales:

- *Multitasking* – which more correctly should be termed Quasi-Multitasking, which is doing more than one activity within a short time span, like texting on the phone while cooking a meal

- *Task Switching* – which is performing one task for a few minutes, interrupting it, turning to another one for a few minutes etc. – such as picking up a phone call interrupting the drafting of a document and then going back to the first or moving to a new task.

5.3.1 Multitasking

If we really attempt to run activities simultaneously, it is making the brain jumping on and off different lines of action, there is a limit of probably less than a handful of them that we can follow. It is thought that this boundary is due to the limited size of our working memory, we simply cannot pay attention to more than to about five items simultaneously [57]. If we force ourselves on more than that, the whole process falls apart, and we essentially are unable to complete any cognitive task. The reason is that above that number, the cognitive processing doesn't just slow down, it breaks entirely apart completely disabling us to proceed, which is mostly attributed to a limit in the size of the brain's working memory. (the processing of information depends on an intensive interplay between parts of the brain that receive and process sensory information and parts that models and predicts the experience – predictive perception. There is a point at which the modelling capacity is simply maxed out and throws the whole system out of synch – Here again, the concept of the brains model coordinated with external information appears, on a much lower level though)

5.3.2 Task Switching

While we typically also speak of multi-tasking when we switch between different task over the course of minutes, the better term to use is task switching. Moving from one state of full focus on one task to another one, it takes up to 10-15 until we are fully immersed into the new one [5]. Furthermore, the more tasks we work on quasi-simultaneously, the more time – and energy – we need for switching [58] and also leads to us getting tired and exhausted faster.

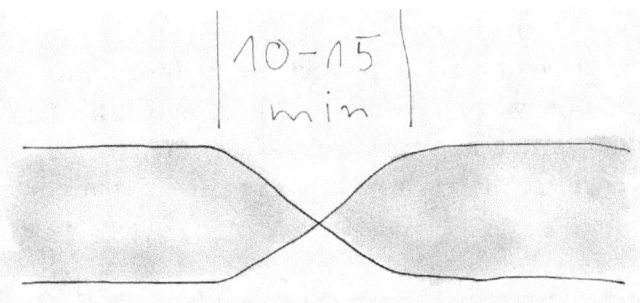

So, cutting down the working day into smaller and smaller pieces reduces drastically the time during which our brains can run at full cognitive capacity, eventually coming to a point at which efficiency is almost zero. In terms of numbers: If we switch 10 times per day from one task to another, we lose about 100 to 150 minutes of our 480 minutes (8 hours) working day. Usually, we move between meetings, phone calls, discussions with colleagues, and 15 min chunks of working at the desk, so the reality is probably much worse. For programming, viewing from the perspective of simultaneous projects, GM Weinberg estimated this loss of time depending on the number of simultaneous projects a programmer is working on:

No. of Simultaneous Projects	Fraction of Time on Project Loss	Loss to Context Switching
1	100%	0%
2	40%	20%
3	20%	40%
4	10%	60%
5	5%	75%

Source: Quality Software Management: Systems Thinking [69]

If we alternatively try to work sequentially, finishing one piece of work, a project, etc. before starting the next one, we gain twofold. On average, tasks are finished earlier, and we save real working time overall. We will see later, how in an organisational context

this makes even more sense. Still, other research has shown, that massive task switching to a certain extent makes us feel good, as we believe in having achieved a lot during the day, however, the actual efficiency is much lower than we imagine [75].

Working with one another

Putting things together, moving from the behaviour of the individuals to how they interact and to new entities of higher-order, groups, organisations networks etc. we have to understand that the limitation of the individual capabilities is a major or even the primary design parameter. Other than in many biological or hierarchical technological networks, the capacities of the edges between the human nodes are limited. There is not a thing like a tree's stem that has the capacity to serve water and nutrients to all leaves or a central artery that guides all the blood to the individual capillaries. Such networks usually have edges that grow in capacity, the closer you get to the centre of the network. Those networks are also called fat tree networks. Here, the dominating design parameter is the terminal unit, e.g. capillaries, wall outlets, faucets etc. [70]. In human networks, there is no such thing as hyper-smart and hyper-fast central nodes with enough capacity to process all information flow within such a network. Processing power, thinking capacity, listening and speaking speed, attention are all different angles to our brain's limits on processing information in a conscious way – at an astonishingly low rate – 20-30 bits/s -, as we have seen (especially when considering what bandwidth in, e.g. mobile phone contracts we already consider as unbearably low) So, while the rate of conscious information processing is already quite low, several

effects are cutting even deeper into the bandwidth
that we have theoretically. These reduce the amount
of information contained in a message (e.g. limited
'newness', ambiguity), disturb the flow of information
(noise), or even produce skewed or false information
being introduced into the process (fallacies, misunderstandings, politics). All that and much more comes
into play when we interact with other people. To
highlight what hurdles and stumbling block we encounter, we will look deeper into the mechanics of
social and organisational interaction

6.1 Structure

Understanding networks better will help us to also
understand communication in organisations better.
How does a specific topology of network influence
the communication it transports? What types of networks are existing, how do they differ in what information they transmit? In this chapter, we will take a
closer look at the theory behind networks. There is
a complete branch of science on that, we will not go
into details, just touch some of the basic concepts

6.1.1 Network topologies

Networks can be of various structural types. How the network ins constructed has significant implications on how communication between its nodes is working. Let us have a look at different general types of networks.

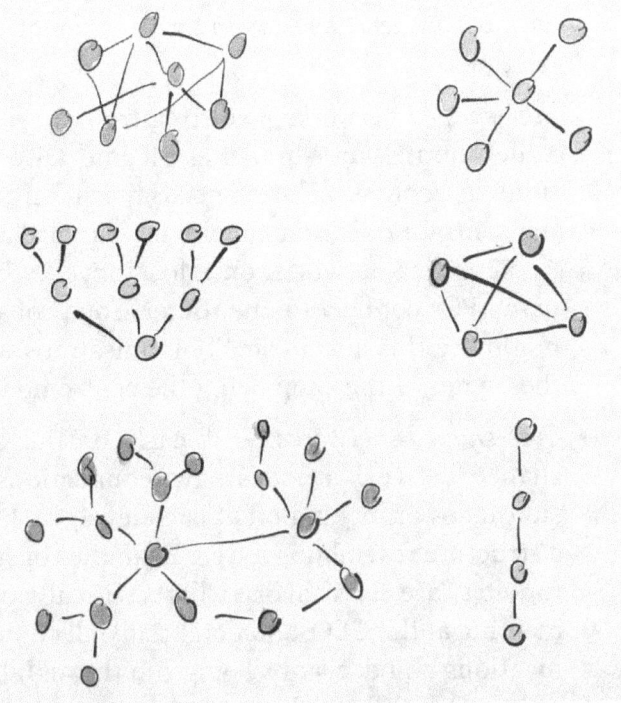

- *Linear networks* – which do not look like a network at all, as nodes are just chained together like a network of information relay stations for optical telegraphs in ancient times. We also can find them in transatlantic communication cables where the information has to be de-noised, amplified and re-transmitted at regular intervals

- *Random networks* – each node has random connections to a random number of other nodes within the network, depending on the randomness, the average number of nodes follows, e.g. a Gaussian distribution or else. (Erdos and Reny) Random networks are very democratic, as most nodes have a similar number of connections.

- *Star-shaped networks* – starting from a central node, the network branches off into all directions. All communication needs to run through the central node. Star topologies, e.g. are used in computer networks on a local level, where many PCs connect to one router. You probably might see this also in small organisations with the owner of the shop being the centre node.

- *Tree-shaped networks* – if each of the star shaped network's nodes have connections to sub-nodes branching off at each level, we have a structure resembling a tree. Examples of such topology are classical org-Charts with all nodes meeting at the CEO, and potentially all communications and decisions being run through him or her. Other examples are trees (of course!) or our cardiac system. There is an important difference between the former and the latter two. While arteries and branches are fat-tree networks, as they increase in size, the closer they are to the central node (to carry more flow, volume, weight), in organisations, the cognitive bandwidth does not increase the closer we get to the CEO. Certainly, a good CEO might also know how to successfully cut out any wasteful communication to maximise his or her usable bandwidth

- *Fully connected networks/Mesh networks* – all nodes are connected to each other. While this works for small groups, we quickly reach a limit as the size of the network increases, when the number of connections will go up by the factorial of the total number of nodes. These types of networks grow into a huge number of connections pretty fast. However, the advantage of such networks is that the maximum distance that a piece of information has to travel from a sender to a receiver is 1. (in the case of a mesh network the limit is how far they can reach out to one another, e.g. in the case of wireless networks this determined by the strength of the senders and the environmental conditions. The distance - the number of hops - that information has to travel can be larger than one and dependent on the location of sender and receiver)

- *Scale-free networks* – in scale-free networks we have a distribution of nodes following the power-law – the number of nodes having a certain number of connections is inversely proportional to the $2_{nd}...3^{rd}$ power of the number of connections – The result is a network ranging from many nodes with a small number of connections to few nodes with a massive number of connections. A prominent example is the internet, where so-called hubs, e.g. Google or Facebook sites, have a huge number of connections while e.g. my homepage and the ones of most other people only have very few. Social networks, biochemical networks, and many other networks in nature follow that principle [29]. Average distances between nodes are kept short as information just needs to reach the next hub to transgress a large portion of the network in just one hop and then just a little to reach their destination. (in turn, those networks also enable super-spreader events in pandemic as we just now could experience).

6.1.2 Types of networks

Networks can also be distinguished by their reason for being. Formal networks usually are planned, generated, and established to serve a specific purpose. They have rules for communication, hierarchies, and clear descriptions of where which node has to be located and what it has to do and whom it speaks to – organisational charts are the most prominent example here. In a typical organisation, the structure is described by an organisational chart, telling us who needs to do what and to report to whom, who tells whom what to do, etc. Usually, the org chart is complemented by project charters describing how within projects, people from different organisational units work together. Finally, a meeting landscape shows us who talks to whom in which meetings. Adjusting an organisational chart requires some analysis and planning and a formal act to change it. There are also a transient forms of formal networks, such as project teams. They are consisting of people from different organisational units across the organisation and are set up for a certain task and are formally disbanded thereafter. Still, project teams that were interacting well also on a personal level might often keep the connection and constitute an informal network thereafter. Informal networks are happening rather than being set up purposefully. You happen to know somebody that knows what you are looking for etc. or you find a part of your family, village, sports club, working at your company or in the same industry. You keep relationships from previous workplaces alive, or you might actively seek membership in some industry association or online business network. Often companies encourage networking through management programs or networking events. In the end, you may have different informal networks that you belong to. These informal networks can be classified by what purpose they serve:

- *"The advice network shows the prominent players in an organisation on whom others depend to solve problems and provide technical information.*

- *The trust network tells which employees share delicate political information and back one another in a crisis.*

- *The communication network reveals the employ-*

ees who talk about work-related matters on a regular basis." [38]

Informal networks help to cut across the boundaries put up by formal networks by providing shortcuts and thus can speed up communication tremendously and also cover up some misconstructions of the formal organisation for a while. Yet, they also carry gossip, half-baked information, and emotions much faster than formal communication paths can keep up to. There is no way of suppressing informal networks. You only can work to make constructive use of them and keep their adverse effects at bay by being aware of their existence and making an effort to understand them (see. Organisational Network Analysis). If you manage this well, the hierarchical structure of your formal networks and the decentral structure of the informal networks merge to make your communication more effective and adaptive to changing challenges. By combining the formal networks with the informal ones, we receive an overall network that is massively connected, the average path-length between nodes is sharply reduced. If used in the right way, this can ensure that information is travelling much faster and with much less effort, thus increasing the efficiency of an organisation. In fact, for some organisations, informal networks might be the only way of remaining operational. a growing internal complexity might render the formal pathways for communication and information flow highly inefficient so that only shortcuts through an informal network lets information reach its destination within a reasonable time-frame.

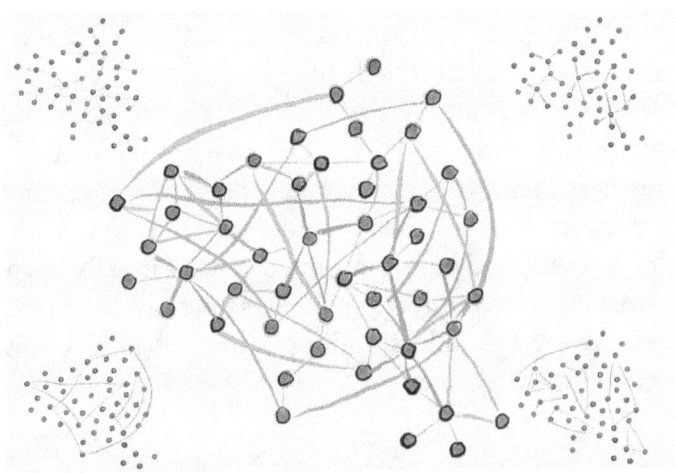

The art lies in orchestrating the various networks in a way that foster overall communication and its efficiency, while all those networks share the same capacities. If, e.g. people feel insecure during a crisis or a difficult economic situation of a company, communication across the trust network can require a good portion of the available capacities and hinder communication about the original purpose of the organisation.

6.1.3 Types of communication

Closely connected to the formal and informal types of networks is the information that flows across them. Facts, opinions, and emotions are flowing across any organisation, through different networks, though. They provide information on the work itself, such as projects, on the processes, and on the people. [60]. No organisation will survive on facts only – if it consists of humans. We will always see opinions and emotions flow around. While formal networks likely mostly transport facts on projects and processes and sometimes (in the case of leadership issues) on people, you will find emotions and opinions mostly in informal networks where people gossip, share rumours, seek advice or understanding – or probably follow their political agenda

6.1.4 The becoming of a network

How is a network starting to exist? To understand better, what information is needed to keep a network in existence, we shall look at the process of networks being born: In plants and animals, all cells start from the same origin and carry the same set of basic knowledge. Differentiation of cells happens by switching on or off certain parts. Depending on the role that the individual cell has to play in the organism, e.g. be a part of the outer skin or make up a part of the liver, or be a leaf cell or a cell in the roots of a tree. Cells only need to know where in the organism they are to know which part of the overall information set they need to use to perform their ‚assigned' task. Most often such signals are communicated in the form of concentrations of various molecules sent out by other cells [39]. In terms of network theory, the class, the nodes are switched to a specific working mode by a little piece of information, telling them to use only certain parts of the complete set of knowledge they carry just like all other cells in the organism – all the necessary knowledge and the encoding of location-specific switching processes being there from the very first moment of their existence (in reality, things are a bit more complicated...). This contrasts sharply with humans, that, of course, carry basic life functions, but need to learn everything else. At the time they come to join an organisation, they may know common standards like language, culture, or may have run through various levels of education calling themselves, nurse, carpenter or engineer. They still do not know how to act as the IT admin of the sales department or as the team lead of marketing and sales of company ABC. To act as a fully functional node they need to know how to play their role, what their position in the network is, what their neighbours and the interfaces are, what information they need to take up from whom and how to process it and how to send it out to which persons, etc. They need to learn all this through fining and taking up the required information and integrate it into their understanding of the organisation – and all over again with every career move or re-organisation or evolution of the tasks.

When setting up a network, we need to answer some basic questions:

- What shall a network look like?
- How large shall it be?

- What is the task of the network?
- How does a node know what its position is in the network?
- How does it know what to do?
- How can it learn to do what it needs to do?
- How does it know whom to talk to and listen to ?

This represents a set of information that needs to be established at the beginning of the existence of any formal network and maintained and adapted throughout its lifetime. An organisation needs to spend cognitive resources on planning its structure on maintaining it and as well on its evolution. Moreover, each node needs to receive information about its position, tasks to be done, and connections to make and on top of that also needs to be fed the knowledge and capability for doing what it is supposed to do – before it even starts spending resources on working on the purpose of the organisation (aka their job). All this eats up cognitive capacity of the organisation – more in times of change and evolution, less while it is maintained in steady-state (occasionally replacing people, fine-tuning etc.). The more dynamic the organisation needs to be the more information for procedures and structure it has to transport through the available pathways – to be more flexible, it needs less and more straightforward rules and structures. Ideally, like stem cells in a body, nodes learn without a central entity steering the process, what role they need to play.

6.2 Collaboration – the team brain

Linking back to what was described above for the individual nodes – the need to build a good model of the world around us, while acknowledging that information is only dripping in -we have to work with the fact that when we intend to build an efficient organisation, team, etc. just communicating the facts of a given situation is not sufficient when we expect to come to meaningful and value-adding conclusions. We have to put significant efforts into sufficiently synchronising the world models, the *'youniverses'* of the people in our organisations regularly – while at the same time ensuring diversity of thought and inflow of new dimensions and ideas. If done successfully, the members of a team share the same world model (in a corporate setting, this shared-world model refers to the corporate world and the world in the immediate surrounding – this is probably what visions and missions, as well as team-building and other workshops, are striving for) and are able to put the model into action when processing information. This sharing of the same world model stretches from merely understanding the processes through knowing the communication network to understanding the needs of the organisation and sharing the same spirit. To build the joint model, each team member brings along his or her expert knowledge, experience, and his or her own understanding so the team can jointly construct the team's world model residing in the team's brain. While the understanding of the world would be synchronised, knowledge will be distributed between the team members, each team member keeping a different portion of knowledge and serving it up to the team as needed. This can work up to a point where the distinction between my brain and your brain is blurred to the extent that I believe to know things that are sitting in your brain, not mine. Rather than having knowledge about a specific topic I have implicit knowledge, I know that you know, yet I treat this knowledge in a similar fashion to mine [63]. Last but not least, people are different and with them the way they assemble their view of the world. Some will have elaborate models on how other people feel, sense the vibrations in the room. Others are perfect builders of a system driven world model or have more of an activity driven model. Knowing the models and modes of thinking of the other members of a team will help to better synchronise, think collaboratively and reduce the amount of meta-communication that is required to get things done and thus free resources for thinking.

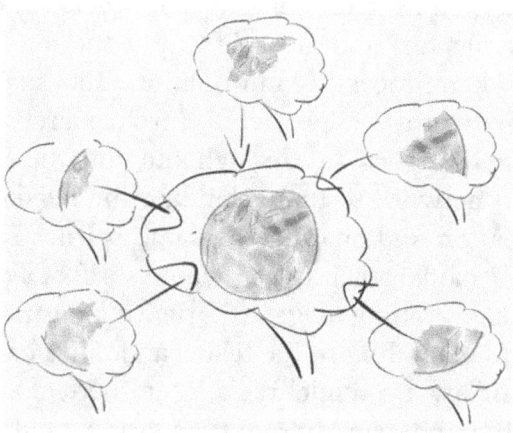

6.3 Fragmented knowledge

In the modern world, no single brain is able to keep all the world's knowledge, not even the knowledge of a single faculty or even of a sub-sub field. Luckily, the reason that our brain is like it is was exactly that. We have our brain for communication and sharing knowledge and using knowledge of our group's members. In almost all settings, we need to rely on the knowledge that other people hold. In the course of division of labour, knowledge is fragmented into smaller pieces and spread across the community or the team. Fragmented knowledge is at the core of human evolution, the one going out to hunt knew a lot about it but probably little about foraging or how to raise the offspring. As seen at the beginning of the text, the purpose of organisations is to manage the division of labour in a way to improve the overall outcome, which almost always results in different parts of the organisation having different knowledge that they hold and apply to live up to their role. Such fragmentation is a precondition to make organisations work, at the same time, it is also endangering their efficient operation. In an organisation, theoretically, for each bit and piece of information and knowledge, there is a division, a department, a team, or a role that is tasked to hold it within, as described in org-charts. Ideally, an org-chart is also a map of the distribution of knowledge in an organisation. In practice, the members of an organisation differ in the degree of their experience, intelligence, motivation, personal interests, availability, etc. Finding the right bit of information sufficiently fast to complete a task is often more challenging than the task itself. Knowing who knows what is crucial to complete a task efficiently. Often, the design of an organisation is causing the fragmentation of knowledge by assigning the ownership of pieces of knowledge that need to be applied jointly into different parts of the organisation, into silos and kingdoms, by restrictions in the access to data or by holding knowledge in a way that requires interpretation before it can be shared. It is not only the spread of knowledge among various sub-units, spreading knowledge across hierarchy can also render decision making slow and faulty. IF the decision power and the knowledge of the subject to be decided upon are too far apart, any decision needs to be preceded by a lengthy and potentially lossy and error-prone communication process. From a network perspective, the number of hops from one node to another that is required to collect the knowledge that is required to complete a given task can be used as a measure of knowledge fragmentation. Ideally, the one that needs the knowledge is having it all at hand 'at his or her fingertips' as IT solutions often promise.

More often than not, the un-official approach is what turns out to be the fastest one. Knowing someone who knows, bypassing all organisationally prescribed pathways is what often makes you getting your work done, actually. Often, organisations are actively fostering the cross-linking, the informal networks through various kinds of networking initiatives, management programs, cross moves, etc. to improve the (informal) information flow. While this

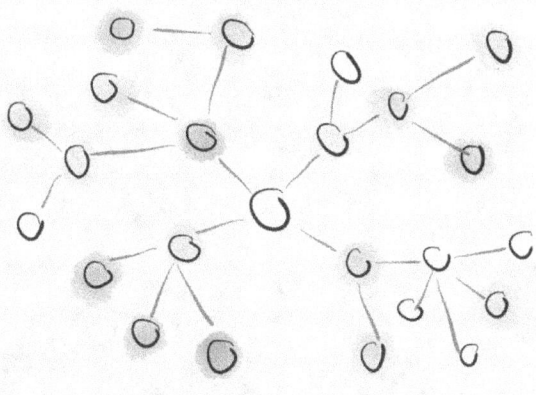

might help to circumvent barriers to information flow put up by the organisational and technical setup, tackling the problem directly might be an even better approach – provide barrier-free access to information and move people closer to each other. After all, information travelling across many nodes in a network eats up capacity, each node needs to take up a request, understand it, find the right recipient and then send it into the right direction – and will do no other work during that time – the limit is 20-30 bit/s. In such a sense, inserting a new node into a dialogue setting will approximately double the cognitive efforts of communication, while introducing noise, ambiguity, and time lag.

Reaching out to others, coordinating, aligning has presumably been one of the drivers for human evolution [18]. Theoretical work showed that the number of people that one person can relate to within a group

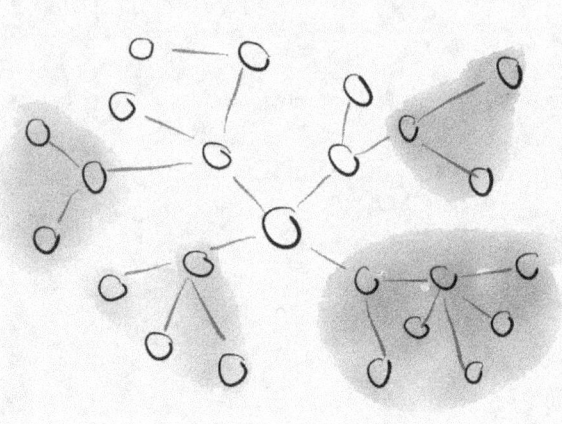

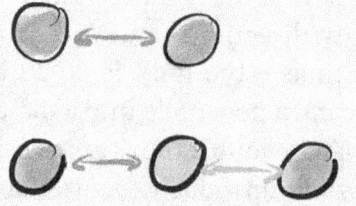

is highly dependent on the cognitive power of the individual brains [15]. Consequently, the more coordination work a group setting requires, the less of the actual (other cognitive) work can be achieved. (There might even be a point at which organisations become self-sustaining....). Luckily, it was also shown, that organising the coordination of communication differently can make us reach out further and manage more coordination with fewer efforts – until we hit the next ceiling.

6.4 Learning and teaching

If knowledge and wisdom are residing inside the individuals' brains, representing the model of the world that each brain has, or being an essential part of it (you either might want to count our unconscious understanding of the world around us to knowledge or not), then learning is the process that feeds information to the brain, combines it with what is already there and incorporate it into our understanding of the world. Following the definitions above, knowledge only resides in an individual's brain, therefore "Information can be transmitted, but knowledge must be induced" [40]. With wisdom building on knowledge, wisdom also cannot be transferred. One can only learn by taking up information – information on facts, on context, on structure, on models, on feelings, etc. Learning by observation or by experience is mainly an interaction between one individual brain and its 'non-conscious' environment and does not necessarily require teaching. When it comes to teaching or training, we often speak of knowledge transfer, which is impossible, strictly speaking. What happens in reality or at least needs to happen is that the teaching brain selects knowledge it wishes to teach, extracts it into information, transmits it, the learning brain takes up the information it receives and adds it to his or her existing knowledge by making meaningful connections to it that are in synch with her world model. Knowledge flow thus could be depicted as an extension to the information flow model of Shannon, (or be seen analogous to Weaver's Levels B and C of the information flow model, adding meaning and intention) – as undertaken by Guglielmo Trentin [66]:

However, both, the teacher's process of extracting information from his or her knowledge as well as the learner's process of making meaningful links to his existing knowledge strongly depends on the model of the world that they live in. The teacher's context might be completely different from the context that the learner has, so might be the knowledge available on both ends, plus all the pitfalls of communication. Essentially we have a situation in which one talks about a supposedly objective fact in his or her outside world while only referencing to his or her inside world-model – that no one else knows or sees – hoping to efficiently add new bits and pieces to the world-model of the other one – not knowing a thing about that one.

Whatever is learned, and no matter how the learning

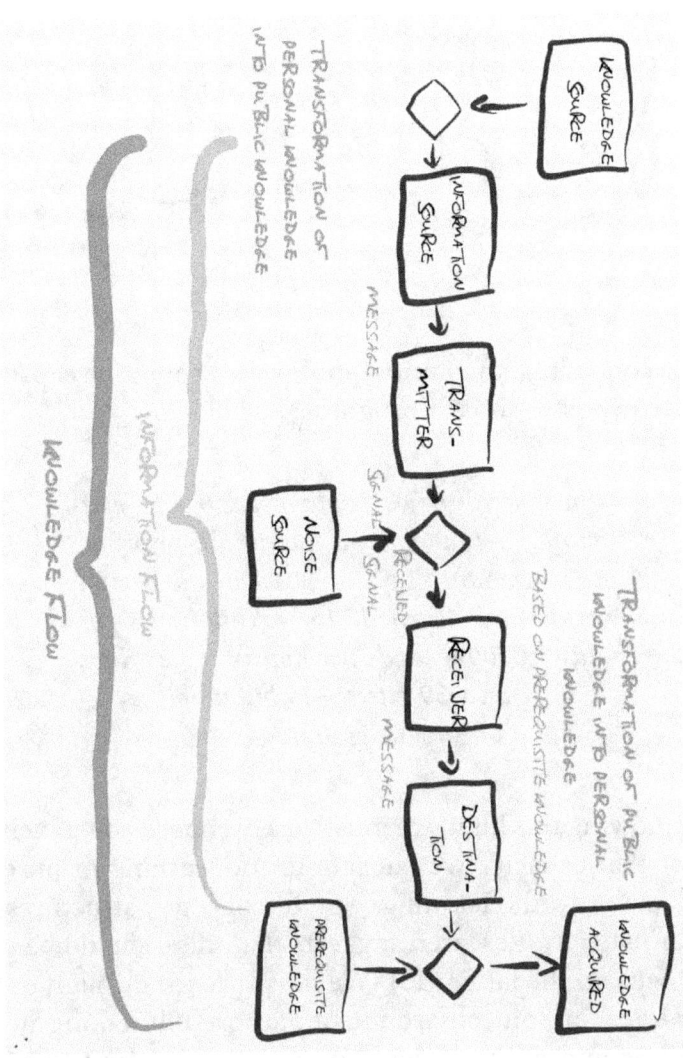

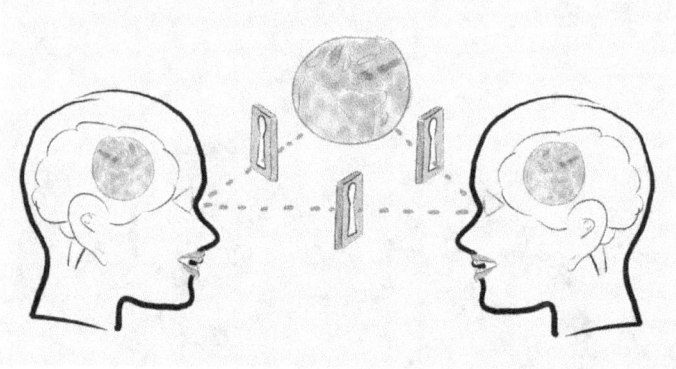

is conducted, the limit of our brain's cognitive capacity persists – it is at roughly 20-30 bits/s.

> *Theoretically, we could even try to estimate how much as a maximum information amount, e.g. a 30-year-old person could have learned: 16 waking hours per day x 3600 seconds per hour x 365,25 days x 30 years x 30 bits/s = 19 billion bits ~ 19 Gigabit or ~ 2,4 Gigabyte*

Knowing this limit, we must wisely choose how much of that capacity we allocate to the learning of pure facts or to the learning, e.g. of concepts, structures, or patterns. Research suggests that there should be a focus on the latter [48]. We mostly learn through experiencing our environment,purposefully taking up ideas and concepts and trying to understand them with our existing world model. If it fits, we find a place in the model to attach the new knowledge to the existing part and continue with an enhanced world model from then on. If what we see or hear does not fit into our world model, we experience cognitive dissonance and initiate a major revamping of our model until the model is consistent again – or we go crazy or turn to beliefs and faiths. We learn best by connecting new information to existing knowledge and thereby establish new knowledge. Facts on their own would be without much of a network to connect to. A brain full of cognitive structures can quickly absorb new information, an empty brain has no connection possibilities and could not really learn. When we learn and teach, the context from which the information is being taught will be almost certainly not be the same as the one it will be absorbed into, consequently, to ensure that everyone in an organisation is working in the similar world model – on the level of the organisation's purpose – training and teaching have to put great efforts into teaching the model structure first before focusing on facts and new information. This starts with the vision and mission of an organisation, its strategy, its culture, and goes beyond the legal and regulatory boundaries that the industry is working under. Only if this is done sufficiently well, people will be able to properly build knowledge and facts into their world model.

6.5 Social Learning

With the size of the brain – the neocortex, to be precise – increasing in the course of human and humanoid development, capabilities such as remembering the past, the concept of time, planning, stories and interactions with others etc. appeared, all of which are capabilities that are not available to most other species at all. This enabled already early humanoids to make use of knowledge outside of their own brain, experiences from the past, as conveyed in stories, beliefs and drawings. Division of tasks and expertise, e.g. planning more extensive interactions in the future, learning from information received from others, communicating learning teaching etc. were evolving. So instead of knowledge being accumulated during lifetime and then disappearing with the death of an individual, knowledge could be preserved and be used as a starting point for the next generations. One generation could now build a platform upon which the next one could base their development on etc. Things needed to be invented only once and then could be used for the rest of the future. Rather than individual learning starting at zero, social learning was possible now. This building up of cumulative knowledge through social learning propelled humanoids into a much faster trajectory than biologic evolution could have ever done.

Rather than the ability to run fast, physical strength or other physical properties, the ability to act as a group and to develop generation-spanning additive cultures now was becoming a decisive factor to human evolution. The human brain (size and structure) and its social capabilities have co-evolved and thus are intrinsically linked. The human brain was built for and through social interaction and does not make

much sense without it. Living within some form of organisation, be it a foraging group, a tribe etc. is an essential part of being human. Modern organisations, however, are stretching this linkage pretty far. While until recently, the evolution has been progressing in a time-frame of tens and hundred thousands of years or even millions of years, man-made organisations have evolved to an incredibly complex level within a few thousand years. It took our brain a long time to be able to actively handle up to 150 individuals (the Dunbar number[24]), now we live in cities of 10.000, 100.000 or many millions of people. Large corporations employ 100.000 people, and more, we have hundreds or thousands of 'friends' on Facebook. All this goes far beyond what our brain is capable of managing in a decent way.

6.6 Perception on an organisational level

An organisation can be seen as an organism that is interacting with its environment. Nodes listening to the outside world, taking up information are its sensory organs, nodes sending out information are its mouth and hands. We can see many of the phenomena that determine what humans can do and can't do on an organisational level: Like individuals, organisations can only take up information to a level of what their nodes can process (i.e. multiples of 20–30 bits/s). You cannot force more information through your interfaces than they can possibly process – you only can hinder them by keeping them busy with other tasks and non-purposeful communication. On the field of perception – 'things are what they are reported to be' (cited from [23]). Whatever you tell your interface nodes to pay attention to, this is what your organisation's sensory organs will pick up. The way such information is perceived by the organisation, in the end, depends on how reporting pathways (i.e. the filtering and consolidation processes) are set up and tuned to through the world model that was set up. The organisation will only listen to information that they expect and judge them against the organisation's world model (strategy, vision, mission, culture). Organisations are also subject to fallacies as we have discussed above. We will see equivalents of the Expectation bias, the Availability bias or the Framing effect in our daily decision making, probably even more in the process of reporting, which can make induced communication patterns grow to become a bomb almost literally when failure culture is tuned into the wrong direction. Some recent examples in the car industry and the banking sector have shown them at work in a drastic manner. Social proof bias is likely looming inside the meeting room whenever a large number of people convene to make some important decisions. We need to work to understand and consciously avoid the filters and fallacies that are at play. What an organisation will see and what it will not see is also determined by its structure, so when setting up an organisation, we need to have the potential fallacies in mind and construct measures to detect and overcome them. (routinely check filtering functions between departments and hierarchies, tap into multiple sources of information, implement short circuits to occasionally bypass filters and calibrate perception etc.)

6.7 Decisions

What is a decision, after all? – A Decision is *'A conclusion or resolution reached after consideration'* [42] – or in other words, in the process of a decision, one takes up some information, transforms it against his or her understanding of the matter, and comes to a conclusion about how to act, what to do next. Models for decision making are many, but most have the components described above – information inflow, information processing, the outcome of the processing, and then finally the action, or at least the intention of acting. A decision that is not resulting in an action does not make much sense, after all. The part of receiving incoming information often is treated differently. While the OODA Model (observe-orient-decide-act) developed by John Boyd [72] separates between observing and orienting, the PDA (perceive-decide-act) loop [28] joins observing and orienting into one single action of perceiving, on the background that any signal that reaches the conscious mind has already been filtered and tested against the individual's 'world model' and thus the two 'O's cannot or should not be treated distinctly. Keeping with the latter, the life of any organism that has some sort of a brain is just an endless sequence of PDA cycles – big ones, tiny ones – each one bringing its life forward by a little bit or by a tremendous leap. On an organisational level, PDA – to perceive, then decide and finally act – is just what has been described above (Section 3.7), the primary purpose of an organisation. Typically though, there is no one big decision that an organisation makes that immediately has an impact. Instead, any action made towards the outside environment has a series of preceding decisions cascading through the organisation, before it actually reaches the outside environment. In an ideal world, the entity or person making a decision collects all the information required, processes it, and then comes to a conclusion on how to act. All information that is needed is available, so decisions can be made with zero uncertainty. In reality, any attempt to act optimally is to be balanced against the cost of doing so-in decision making it is the cost of acquiring and processing the information and the time required to do so, both of which as we have seen are tapping into the scarce resource of the conscious processing capacity of the brain. Acquiring and processing all information available and required for a decision would take unlimited resources and unlimited time. Consequently, real-world decisions are always bounded by the resources and time available and thus always come with some uncertainty of really being optimal and never are perfectly rational.

In organisations, decisions are often not made by individuals, but rather by groups of individuals, such as project teams, committees, boards, etc. Here the individual uncertainties meet differing perceptions, levels of knowledge, politics, and cultural backgrounds. This makes group decisions on complex topics a totally statistical endeavour (see also [68] :

- No group member has all information that is optimally required

- Each group member has a different set of limited information

- Each one decides on his own set of values and world model, culture, etc.

- Each one's perception is differing from the others and leads to a different interpretation of the same facts

- Each one has different dependencies, goals, and drivers

- Discussing facts and interpretations is subject to common communication noise and fallacies

While any decision is subject to uncertainties, group decisions are even more so. We probably can assume, that there is some probability that repeating a decision process with the same group members at a different point in time will lead to a different decision, with all other things being equal. The larger the group, the higher the uncertainty of the decision. Decisions by large groups have another detrimental effect, with each member having had a small part of the argumentation and decision process, the feeling of responsibility goes down too, and with it the willingness to stand to decisions that were made. This might be one reason why the OSS (predecessor of the CIA) saw routing decisions through committees of a specific size and re-routing them a while later as an effective tool in undermining the efficiency of foreign organisations [52].

Another aspect to be considered, albeit on a lower cognitive level, is that decision-making is a resource that is not endless, it could be shown that it is actually a depletable resource, we only have the willpower to make a certain number of decisions during the day, so that at the end of a decision-heavy day we tend to go for easy decisions, e.g. opt for the status quo rather than a change. [30] This so-called decision fatigue essentially means that each decision uses some mental energy that is needed to maintain a certain level of self-control to work on long term goals rather than follow our basic needs and urges short term. The more complex or important a decision is, the more mental energy is used. The mental energy is not used by preparing for a decision but rather by the decision itself. Once the mental energy is used up, it will be hard to keep ourselves from following our basic needs and emotions. [53][7] resulting in us likely choosing the easy option, follow stereotypes, or just pick the 'do nothing' option if available. Interestingly, a little rest or even just eating can restore our reservoir and put us back on track [22]. We can also try to avoid decision fatigue by avoiding unnecessary decisions, this is supposedly also the reason for Steve Jobs always wearing a black sweater.

6.8 Innovation and creativity

Innovation and creativity are heavily used terms in modern organisations and at the same moment somewhat ill-defined. Both terms depend on individuals having ideas. So, what is an idea? In his book "A technique of producing ideas"[76], James Webb Young ventured to define:

1. *an idea is nothing more or less than a new combination of old elements*

2. *the capacity to bring old elements into new combinations depends largely on the ability to see relationships*

Interestingly, this understanding has an analogy on the neuronal level, as described in the words of Steven

Johnson [31]:

"A good idea is a network. A specific constellation of neurons—thousands of them—fire in sync with each other for the first time in your brain, and an idea pops into your consciousness." and *"The adjacent possible is a kind of shadow future, hovering on the edges of the present state of things, a map of all the ways in which the present can reinvent itself."*

One thing that these definitions tell us immediately is the realisation that innovation strongly depends on existing (old) elements being there. If there are no existing elements, there are no ideas to be generated. Recalling the section about the nodes above, the old elements refer to the bits and pieces of the world model in an individual's brain. To have ideas and thus drive innovation, we need a good number of concepts of the world being available in our own brains. The more such 'old elements' we have available in our world model, the more we can combine them, the more relationships we can see. To be creative, to have ideas, we need to have as many elements available as possible [37]. If we want to be creative, we consequently need to work on building up the number of elements we have available. I.e. we need to know a lot, to have seen a lot, to have worked to understand a lot and to spent time on thinking on relations between the things we see and experience. Scaling up to the organisational level, to drive innovation and the generation of ideas, we need to combine the brains of many people and make use of all the elements contained within all the brains. How well this can work all depends on having an efficient way of sharing the bits and pieces of the world models of the individual team members, on the techniques used to manage communication of the elements, setting aside capacity to process it in the individual's brains and find an efficient means to sharing the outcome again. The more diverse the individual brains are (the diversity of backgrounds, experiences, cultures) the larger a thinking space the team can span, the more the dimensionality grows. However, all that the individual brains can bring to the table, needs to have been in the brains before, so it is not the number of the people you engage in the process, it is how sophisticated a model of the world they have built up, and of course how diverse those models are.

6.9 Asynchronous working

In most settings, these days, we collaborate with many people across our organisation, link to people from other organisations, time zones, and cultures and typically work on more than one topic any given day or hour. This almost inevitably leads to a situation where we work on a topic or project up to a certain point, then try to call a colleague or email her to ask for some missing piece of information or ask for a decision, etc. More than often, we will not have an answer immediately, our colleague needs to check on something before being able to answer or is booked until later this week or promises to call back or reply by mail. While waiting, we pick up another task – that we will interrupt at a similar point -, answer some overdue request or do some low priority work or else. In the end, we, but also all the others that we are working with, are kept in a state between waiting and juggling with numerous different lines of action and an increased amount of time we spend chasing information and timelines. The latter, as we have seen in the chapter on task switching, is wasting bandwidth and energy and lets us produce results much later than a more focused way of working.

Resulting from that, people spend a lot of time waiting for the completion of sub-tasks of others, these tasks will get finished much later. Just compare the time people are working on any given workflow with the time it takes from start to finish – it will likely be a ratio of minutes or a few hours vs weeks and months. Besides, everybody will have more simultaneous tasks on his table than needed and healthy, spend more time on switching between them, more time to follow up and send around steering and control information. At the same time, things take longer, and the organisation gets done less. We quickly get into a feedback loop that makes things worse and worse

6.10 Organisational Efficiency

How do we measure the efficiency of an organisation (an organisation only processing information, the typ-

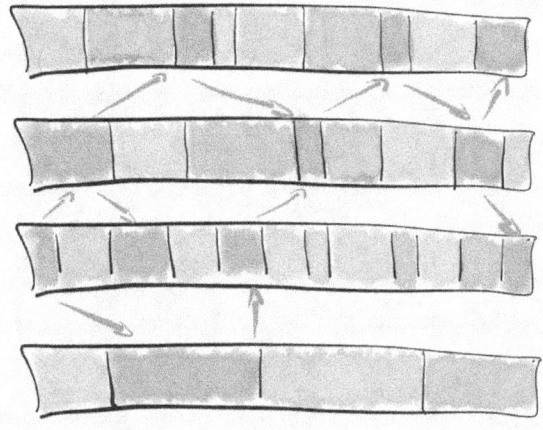

ical office setting)? As outlined initially, the purpose of an organisation is to take up information from the environment, process it, and emit information in a way that generates a benefit towards the purpose of an organisation itself. The efforts that are put into this process in the light of their outcome can be used as a measure of the efficiency of the very organisation – leaving out the other terms characterising a process – energy and matter, as those play a secondary role in the typical office organisation.

All the information that is received and processed by the nodes inside of the organisation (all) is the effort put into the process, all information that is sent back to the outside of the environment (red arrows/ outgoing arrows) is the effect – not considering the quality of the information at this moment. Consequently, the information efficiency of an organisation can be described as:

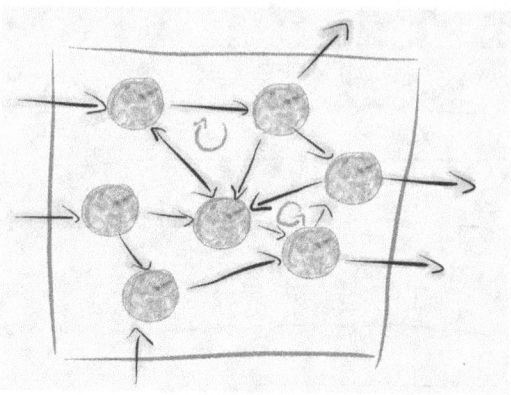

$$\text{Information efficiency} = \frac{\text{information sent out from an organisation}}{\text{information processed within an organisation}}$$

The only information that immediately can create value towards the purpose of the organisation, while all the information that is transported or transformed within the organisation, between its nodes or stored somewhere cannot create any value directly. In reality, it is quite difficult to put exact numbers behind the terms relating to information in the formula above, so we also may think of the efforts and time put into processing and communicating. If we replace in the calculation the information sent out with the actions that we strive for to induce with the outbound communication, we also can calculate the organisational effectiveness: We will leave it at that, as we will not

$$\text{Organisational efficiency} = \frac{\text{actions induced in the environment}}{\text{information processed within an organisation}}$$

look much deeper into how the actions in the outside environment are actually induced. From both views, however, one simple rule of thumb can be derived: information that never leaves the office building is worthless! The amount of internal and external communication and their ratio clearly is one parameter that significantly influences how efficient an organisation can be. Surely other factors, such as what is communicated and how is it communicated also play an important role.

So, how is the size of an organisation linked to the efficiency of the organisation? As we have seen, forwarding information, finding the right person to answer a specific question is eating up cognitive capacity within an organisation, the more hops from node to node a request is travelling, the more capacity is used. The capacity of a communication network comes down to the capacities of the individual nodes. Each communication uses some capacity of some node. An email sent to 10 instead of 2 people, a meeting with 6 instead of 3, etc. all use up capacity – 20-30 bit/s per person! While it is almost impossible to calculate the precise throughput of a given organisation, we can try to work out some estimates how and into what direction the overall throughput develops when we change the size of an organisation by looking at estimates made in related domains, such as communication technology For example, in computerised communication networks, for random wireless meshed networks, the throughput is depending on the number of nodes within the network, the assumption being a randomly meshed network where all nodes speak to all other nodes in their reach. Here we can find that, roughly put, the specific throughput rate of such a network can be described by the following characteristic [43]: We see that there is a negative correlation, the specific throughput rate

$$\text{throughput rate} = \Theta \left(\frac{1}{\sqrt{n \cdot \log n}} \right)$$

goes down when the number of nodes goes up and would reach zero in infinitely large networks. I have to contend though, that a precise calculation of information throughput in such settings Is not possible to date, as current network science shows. [19] Transferring this mechanism into an organisational network, we at least can estimate the characteristic of efficiency loss dependent on its size:

An organisation of 100 People has a cognitive processing capacity of 100*30 bit/s (assuming it is comprised of brilliant people only, we use the upper limit of our capacity rate) enabling the entire organisation to process 3000 bit/s or 3 kb/s.

Doing the calculation for a network setting, we find that if everybody were to communicate randomly with everybody within reach, the capacity would decline by a factor of about 14! So, in this extreme scenario, the remaining effective capacity would be just 214 bit/s – which is about what just seven people could achieve in an ideal environment. In reality, indeed, the drop is less drastic as communication is not entirely random and more intensive within departments and teams and less across the boundaries of organisational structures. What remains is the indication that the larger the organisation gets, the lower the specific throughput is. An organisation where everybody communicates with everybody through many hops could serve as the worst case in our estimation. (The extreme case would be an organisation that could be kept busy just by circulating information internally with no need for outside stimulus – we probably all have made corresponding assumptions). It also tells us that designing the organisation in a way that access to information requires only a small number of nodes will increase the efficiency of an organisation. The ideal state, after all, is the whole network/organisation acting like one single node able to perform all given processing tasks and not needing to align, share and agree, thus knowing it all and not requiring anything and anyone else:

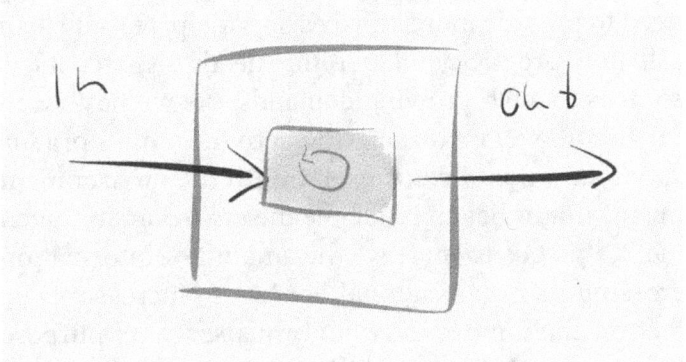

6.11 Growth

What happens, when an organisation grows? How does its main characteristics change, if they change at all? Is a large organisation just an exact copy of a small one scaled up by a factor of X? Is it more efficient, or less? When we look at nature or even artefacts such as cities, we find that there are some scaling laws, that are based on the basic functions of their terminal units, such as capillaries in the bodies of humans and animals, whose size and distribution are in turn determined by the diffusion coefficients of Oxygen and Carbon dioxide respectively, or the average power connection point to households etc. [70] Is there a similar design principle at play when it comes to organisations?

When an organisation grows, it typically does so to adjust to or anticipate a growing need for its activities (according to the purpose of the organisation). It may need to provide more services or anticipate that it can sell more products and therefore needs to match its resources to such growing demands. As we have seen further above, increasing the activities of an organisation and the effect it exerts onto the environment means that it has to influence the environment much more, it needs to increase the amount of information crossing its organisational borders to increase its effect on the environment and thus serve its purpose to a maximal degree. With a fixed, limited amount of information that a node on the boundary of the organisation can process, growth is only possible, if the numbers of those nodes go up. More information coming into the network require also an increase in processing power. Nodes inside the network mostly are tasked with processing the incoming information through multiple steps of analysis and decisions into outgoing information that in the end is resulting in actions/activities induced in the environment. So, we need to also increase the number of those respective nodes. Additionally, administrative- and support-, as well as adaptive-tasks, will need to manage the additional flow of information. All those steps require additional capacities, too. Depending on the setup of the organisation, the organisation can scale linearly or sub linearly (meaning: increased or stable efficiency, respectively) or lead to a point where almost all additional resources go into managing and handling the flow of information rather than processing it (like adding signalmen and shunters to a railroad network rather than engine-men and conductors) and running many things in parallel makes task switching the main activity. When we try to channel all crucial information processing through a few nodes and those nodes only having a finite capacity, more pre-processing, information reduction, etc. is needed and potentially will lead to a situation in which bottlenecks limit the throughput or faulty pre-processing leads to wrong decisions. Which in the end also leaves the subsequent nodes with a lack of information. Simply put, to support the 'surface' (which in case of a 2D sketch below example is named correctly as perimeter) to the outside in a given organisational setting, the growth of the supporting structure inside typically has a higher exponent than the surface itself (i.e. grows faster) comparable to the perimeter of a circle growing linearly with the radius, while the area grows squarely (power-law). While the area-perimeter relation is just a depiction of the principles at play, analogies from biological systems show that certain networks tend to be space-filling – they fill the

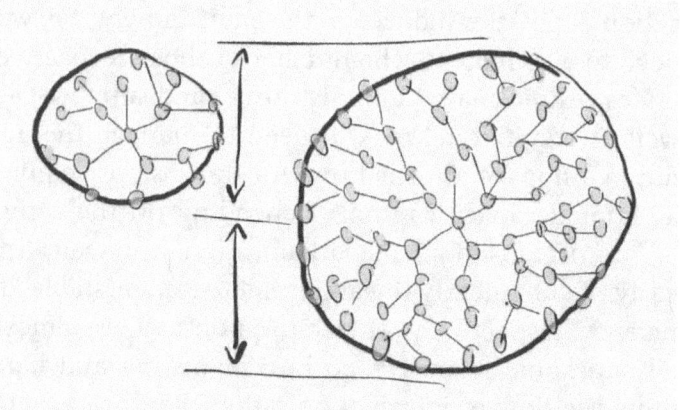

available space [70]. In organisational theories, such
effect was also stated by Parkinson [54] or translated
to or metaphor of the circle – if more interaction is
needed, the perimeter is grown as a result. The additional area will be filled with additional nodes, even
without a specific need or reason. In this analogy,
doubling the effect of the organisation, as represented
by the nodes on its outer perimeter requires quadru-
pling the nodes managing the internal information
flow inside of it – that is, if one keeps the design parameters constant, such as span of control, partition,
or reporting structure. Consequently, in such a case,
the organisational efficiency goes down. This mani-
fests in the right side of a logistic curve typed development of efficiency the is observed when an organisation grows. As an organisation starts to evolve, it initially is gaining efficiency by harnessing the division
of labour, tools, new processes, etc.- the output grows
faster than the number of people. In the following
stage, efficiency stays constant, 10% more turnover
means 10% more people up to the point where the or-

ganisation runs into bottlenecks, the effort needed to manage the information flow eats up significant capacities, and the system grows sub-linearly. This was observed by Geoffrey West, who examined the data of S&P 500 companies concluding that companies scale sub-linearly, likely due to rules and processes starting to dominate over innovative powers [70].

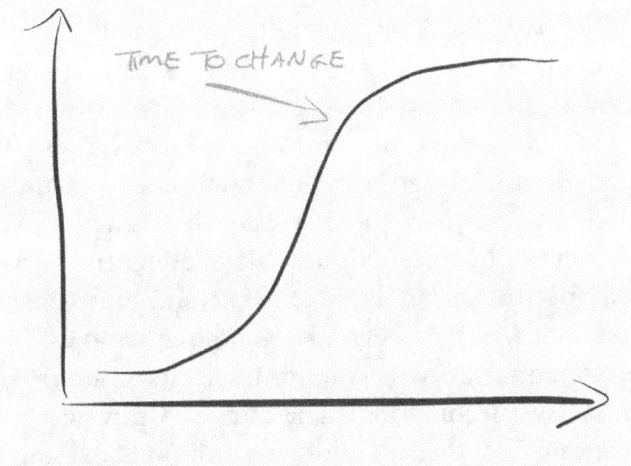

This levelling off of the curve is the point in time that signals to urgently change the organisational setup (or to live with the fact that over time your organisation can be kept busy just by shuffling information around without any need of external interaction...). Re-organising the organisation essentially means to re-organise the information flow within. More bandwidth to channel information from the outside through the organisation's internal workings and releasing it to the outside world again, will decrease the efforts to handling it and leave more room to process the information increase the bandwidth across the organisation. Basically, we see here, among other effects, the manifestation of the fact, that the size of a human network is limited by the capacity of the individual brains' power. The ideal state, lossless, cognitive processing and communication is merely providing the upper ceiling. Other effects, like non-equilibrated resource distribution, lack of knowledge, intercultural difficulties, etc. further lower that ceiling. Only a change of the way we work together, of the basic parameters, a purposeful re-design of the information flow can make us break through such a ceiling and enable the organisation to grow further – and hitting the next ceiling eventually. organisations that try to grow exponentially need to undergo such changes ever more frequently as they move up that curve to closely follow the exponential curve by leaving further me logistic curve and jump onto the next one (And should understand that what looks like exponential growth is quite likely just the first half of an overarching logistical curve. A physical world like ours just doesn't allow for unlimited exponential growth...)

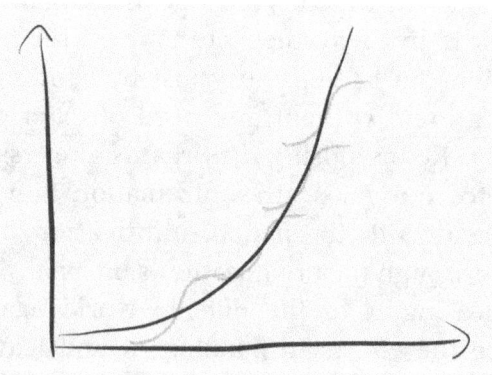

6.12 Complexity

How does a complex world influence the inner workings of an organisation? What is complexity, after
all? How does it influence our individual interaction
with the world? First, we should try to understand
the term 'complex'. While used often in today's world,
it turns out that everybody seems to have a different
definition of the word complex. For this text and our
focus on organisations and communication, I will use
the word complex to describe something (a system)
that is consisting of a large number of related and interacting units, the nature of those relations and interactions only being imperfectly known and impossible to be described sufficiently by rules. Examples are
the world itself, but also large organisations, weather,
living cells, human behaviour, etc. Often complexity
('*the world is getting increasingly complex*') is used as
a synonym or in context with volatility, uncertainty,
and ambiguity (see VUCA-world, a term being introduced in the late 80s by the US War College to describe the post-cold-war world) [73]. Probably complexity can best be described as something complicated, lots of bits and pieces that are interacting in
a way that we do not nearly understand and can predict. Complexity needs to be viewed from two angles:
internal complexity and the external complexity.

- *Internal complexity* refers to how the organisation itself is set up, how many interactions and
  possible stated does it have, does it follow simple rules, etc. This kind of complexity can be

influenced by the organisation itself and determines how the organisation interacts with external complexity.

- *External complexity* refers to the outside world that an organisation interacts with. It is described by the number of units, the interactions, rules/laws, requirements, etc. that the organisation faces in its environment. The organisation has to live with the fact that it has to deal with an outside environment that it does not fully understand and it thus cannot model and also cannot change much.

What challenges does complexity pose to an organisation? The organisations' world model is built on what it sees and understands and interacts with, with information flowing in, limited by the capacity of the nodes listening to the outside world. It is housed within and shared and split between all brains of the organisation's members and organisational documents. Building the model and synchronising it sufficiently is a process that requires cognitive communication capacities before we even can think about capacities available to put it into use. (→organisations need to organise the process in a most effective way to build a sufficiently good model with as little capacities as possible – aka learning, team- and mindset-building, process design, etc.) Adding the fact that the world is not static and the speed of change is accelerating when it comes to technology, society, communication, etc. there needs to be a constant inflow of new information leading to the permanent update of the model that further strains the information processing capacity. The way an organisation sets itself up for the process of building and maintaining its model of the world is determining a lot how much of the capacities are used. Typically, organisations try to match the external world with internal structures – customers/marketing and sales – suppliers/sourcing – regulators/legal and also match it at a much more detailed level, too. Communication flows happening alongside those lines. This may work well in structured, stable, and lucid environments. The 'world model' is built once and only requires gentle adjustment to slowly shifting settings. The more dynamic and diverse the outside world becomes, the more difficult it becomes to incorporate and keep current the information representing the outside world and adjust structures accordingly. organisational adjustment processes being not very fast typically, you would find yourself easily in a situation where the lag between the inner world model and the real world is rendering your organisations' world model often much useless. Trying to match an increased outside complexity by increasing the inside – the organisational – complexity is not the way to go. A more complex inner structure requires more coordination work, average distances will increase, use more bandwidth probably even more than just the sheer growth would do (see section 6.11 on growth). With the cognitive capacity of the organisation's members being limited, this will at one point create a situation in which the organisation is choking on its own complexity before it can even deal with the outside complexity. This is a situation where only a fundamental change in the organisational setup and of the underlying principles can provide a way out. Instead of adding complexity, the organisation needs to move towards simplicity, less structural information in its own setup, fewer rules, more guidance, shorter pathways, faster decisions, etc. Often, planning and budgeting processes are seen as a way to safely steer the organisation through a stormy future, cutting swathes through the jungle of complexity following the paradigm – better planning – less complexity. However, especially once the planning process becomes ever more sophisticated to keep up with increasing (external) complexity we essentially only increase internal complexity and give away flexibility to adapt to what cannot be planned for anyway – the future [46]. So, instead of detailing out scopes of responsibilities, interfaces, and reporting pathways, just define the domain that is in focus, ensure that all required capabilities are available to a given task or project, and put people to work that define themselves how to collaborate. Focus on creating a framework that allows the organisation to adjust itself to whatever structure is needed in a given moment. This will ensure that white spots are filled and covered through the internal alignment of the team. Besides, this approach also provides for a richer work life and a better feeling of control to the ones being given the freedom to align with their peers on their work within such frame and hopefully avoids some of the alienation of work [44] that is seen when task are atomised too much.

A famous example are the *'desire paths'* – instead of pre-planning the pathways for people to move around campus at a point when not even the build-

 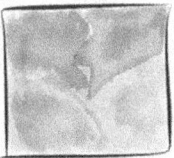

ings were readied, one college in the US choose to wait until people actually started walking around and choosing the paths of their desire – and only then to fix and pave them. [67] So, they pragmatically – and smartly – used the information coming from the actual behaviour of the real world, rather than spending a lot of effort on theorising and assuming things. Resulting from this is a system that is putting resources (walkways) where they are needed and prevent waste and harm (damaged lawns). (in the domain of quality systems: if the easiest and obvious way is also the correct one, there will be dramatically fewer deviations). Here's an example of how improper planning leads to unplanned deviations :

Lastly, the design of processes has a tremendous impact on the level of complexity that is built up within an organisation. While division of labour is a necessity and a prerequisite for assembling people into organisations, it also increases the need for communication. This can reach a level where internal processes est up all of the available bandwidth without creating much of the organisations purpose. Smartly setting up processes that require just little communication are a way to avoid this. One well known example is the Kanban system developed at Toyota where e.g. empty boxes are a very clear and simple signal for a production need [65]. Communication that is just not needed is the best way to prevent a waste of the scarce resource of cognitive bandwidth of the people in the organisation.

Analysis

7.1 organisational Network Analysis (ONA)

An organisation should try to understand its inherent network setup.

- Who speaks to whom?
- How much is the official (org chart) network used.
- What roles play the informal networks
- Which ones are in existence?
- Who are the people to know, the bridges, the gatekeepers, where are the bottlenecks?

There are specific roles within a network that deserve a more detailed view, as they are important in large scale networks. How many of them are present, where they are placed, how efficient or inefficient they act, determines how the whole network is functioning. In the following, the main roles are described:

- "*Bridges*: Bridges are very similar to Liaisons but with one major difference. A Liaison is not associate with any group, but a bridge is connected with a group. This occurs when roles serve a similar purpose, but their connections are different.

- *Gatekeepers*: A Gatekeeper is somebody who monitors what information to pass on. A person can be at a company for fifteen years and still learn something new every day. However, that person may be the gatekeeper of information for a new employee. Instead of trying to cram all the information, there is into a new employee brain, a gatekeeper will monitor what needs to be said. [...]

- *Stars*: These people are also known as the opinion leader and will typically have an influence on the job with group members. They may not have an official role, but there are stars everywhere. Someone may be viewed as a supervisor because of that person's behaviour. If they are admired by other employees and have a positive commanding presence, they may be regarded as a star.

- *Cosmopolites*: Also known as boundary spanners, these people have high communication with the outside world or the organisation's environment, and also may link one organisation with another. This could be a transportation department that deals with multiple shipping and export or import companies.

- *Isolates*: This is what it sounds like- being isolated. There are different forms of isolates in a company. An employee can be isolated from a meeting because he has nothing to add. Then there are possession isolates; for example, a sales representative for a large company could be considered an Isolate. They are disconnected from the internal network of a company and focus on the customer. The problem is they are often the last to know of policy changes, or products being on back-order or becoming obsolete." cited from [25]

Again – we are speaking of organisations that just process information, the only thing that counts is how fast and efficient we can turn information from the outside into decisions and actions influencing the outside world to our benefit.

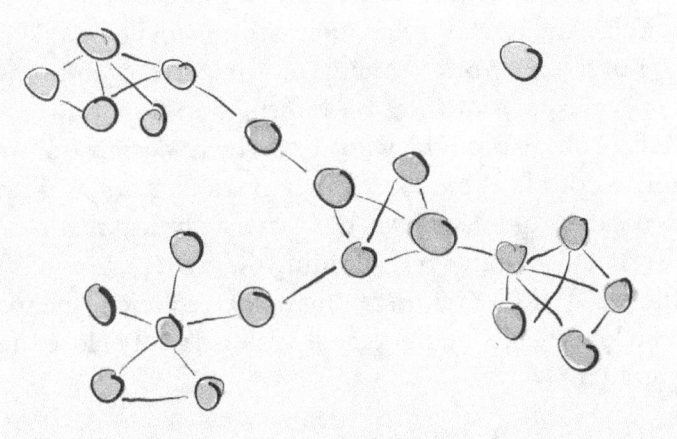

different roles in a communication network and how they are related – according to [25]

To find out how your network is actually working, organisational network analysis can deliver a lot of information and insights. ONA can be performed through questionnaires, asking who people speak to regularly, which are their primary sources of information, and what official interactions, meetings, etc. they participate in. With most of the communication being performed through electronic means, much of the data is already there, e.g. a Microsoft dominated environment will hold much of what is needed to understand the communication flow on the Exchange Servers and Skype or MS Teams activity logs (and would produce many sleepless nights for the data protection and privacy officer!). The benefit is that you might be able to, e.g. pinpoint bottlenecks in the transmission of information from one part of the organisation to the other and work to strengthen the respective node and add others to increase the bandwidth. And by this avoid, that one person being taken out of the network (leaving the company, promotion, etc.) makes your internal information flow put to a halt. You also might want to actively design the information flow, by consciously installing nodes with dedicated roles (which is not just a technical manoeuvre, but also requires HR finding the right person with the right skills) or installing some technical means (can knowledge management systems really close the gap here?)

The figure below shows an example based on public data from the Enron email corpus, a dataset that is often used for network visualisation and machine learning examples. [41], *(you can find it at:http: //www.cs.cmu.edu/~enron/ and http://www.cis.jhu.edu/ ~parky/Enron/, the graph was produced with GEPHI 0.92).* We see in the figure, how, based on their email exchange, different nodes in the organisations' network are connected. Thick lines represent a close interaction – i.e. many email contacts, light lines only a few email touch-points. The size of the circles depicts the overall traffic through these nodes. Colours point out clusters of nodes having a close relationship. Based on such visualisations and the underlying calculations, one can learn much about the fragmentation of the network, single nodes channelling traffic through them and groups that are somewhat isolated from the rest of the organisation.

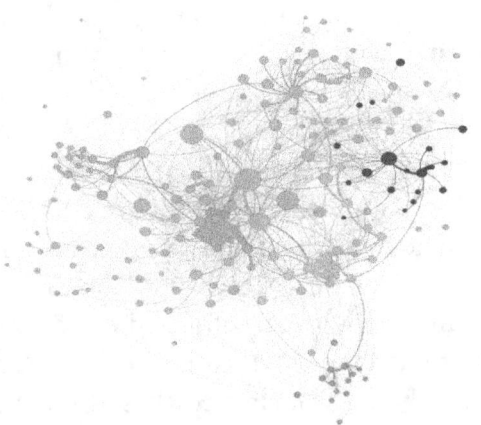

Network analysis based on Enron email dataset

7.2 Flow Analysis

To get a first understanding of how much communication is happening within your organisation and to

get a first hunch on the effectiveness of the organisation, you could turn to your IT and have a look
into their network statistics. You will find the hourly,
daily monthly, etc. statistics of your email traffic,
likely split into external traffic and internal traffic. In
environments with unified messaging, you probably
would have also have some useful statistics on phone
calls, chats etc. Typically, there are even more detailed statistics available that you could get hold of if
allowed by the applicable data protection regulations
and policies (see the comment on MS environment
in section 7.1 above). The relation of internal and
external communication – leaving out the vast portion of spam emails – gives you a first glimpse on the
organisational efficiency as defined above. To establish a more robust picture, we need to understand not
only the gross amount of data that is sent across the
network but its information content. While we will
hardly be able to distinguish useful information from
useless or false information without looking into each
sentence and file with an informed mind, we can approach this challenge by looking into the newness of
information being transmitted (based on the understanding that information that is already known by
the receiver is not information). In digital information flows, we often find repeated information that
is added due to some requirements or standards to
each message that is sent. Emails typically contain
some disclaimer/footer, word processor files and pre-
sentation files contain some headers with identifica-
tion and processing information, all of which are the
same within each instance and therefore do not represent some new information. Furthermore, drawings,

pictures and schematics contain a lot of white-space, repetitive patterns etc. that do not add information bit by bit. We need to remove all this duplicate and non-information before we can judge the information content that a message contains. We further must distinguish between the gross data and its information content. The gross amount of data is describing how much, e.g. a reader must read to take up the message the information content describes how much information the reader actually takes up in that process. As we have seen in 4.1, English language per se has a redundancy of about 50% meaning that 100 bits of an average English text contains no more than 50 bits of information. 50% is the upper limit, as we have to consider repetitive words and content, language being reduced to a specific domain and therefore using a limited number of different words etc. To judge the information content, we must consider all that and establish how much information as a minimum is needed to describe the complete information contained in the given message. What we are looking for is also known as the Kolmogorov complexity. The Kolmogorov complexity is the shortest representation of a given informational object [36], which is essentially the information content of such object. When doing so, we firstly must understand the questions we try to answer based on the available communication data. While the previous section was looking at who speaks to whom and how often, a quantitative analysis of the information flow looks into how much information is flowing within the network, such as:

1. Communication between two nodes

2. Internal communication

3. Inflow and outflow of individual nodes

4. Communication across the organisations boundaries, inflow and outflow

While a qualitative analysis reveals a lot of the structure and the complexity of an organisation, it does not tell us much about the cognitive load that each node has to carry and how this load is distributed across the network and over time. let us have a look into the individual approaches in more detail:

1. **Communication between nodes:** We can determine how much gross and net information has been shared between two nodes in a dialogue. As derived measures, we could calculate the net directional information flow, the density of the flow in each direction, the cognitive load of each node resulting from the dialogue etc. The tricky part here, as with all other items to follow, is that the time-span that we look at has a high impact on the calculation. If it is too small, all the information that we look at within the specific time-frame would be new and therefore would be counted as net information, if it is too large, on the one hand it becomes impractical to calculate, on the other hand, we probably must consider that people are not remembering what they have been told long ago and therefore consider such information as new. (Factoring in 'forgetting' might be

an interesting and challenging endeavour.)

2. **Internal communication:** A measure to calculate internal communication efficiency would be to compare the cumulative gross amount of all emails, calls, meetings etc. to the newness contained within them. Postulating that e.g. information that has to travel far across different nodes by being relayed multiple times (thus each time adding a duplicate of such information to the transmission of information at each relay node) is not really purposeful with respects to an organisation's goal, we could estimate the fraction of purposeful communication and information generated (or dug up from some long-forgotten or secretive archive) within the organisation in the respective time-frame

3. **Inflow and outflow of a given node – or sub-unit:** Comparing the gross and net information inflow and outflow would enable us to calculate the information generation activity of this node. We would be able to identify primary relay nodes, generative nodes etc. (or probably even be able to calculate time lag etc...)

4. **Communication across the organisations boundaries:** One important outcome of such calculation would be the information efficiency as described under 4.10., the ratio between the information content leaving the organisa-

tion and all the gross information transmitted within the organisation – which is actually a tightening of that definition as not the amount but the content of communication is in the numerator here.

$$\text{Information efficiency(2)} = \frac{\text{information content sent out from an organisation}}{\text{(information processed within an organisation)}}$$

To calculate the information content of a message (or file, etc.) within a good approximation, we can make use of a suitable compression algorithm. Many commercial compression tools allow the adjustment of parameters, such as window size, dictionary size, compression ratio etc. leading to good and stable results. An algorithm performing fairly well has turned out to be PPM (Prediction by Partial Matching) [9]. Theoretically, to get closest to the real information content, you would need to look at all information that has ever been transmitted in the given context across all channels and then compress it by removing all duplicate information. Pragmatically, as already described above, we need to find a reasonable level of practicability and timeframe to make it work and yield initial results

7.3 Further analysis

With natural language processing advancing swiftly, further analysis would be possible, regarding the content, meaning and also the tone of communication or the sentiments transmitted in it. The previously described analysis processes were examining the structure of a communication network (ONA) or the quantitative information flows (information flow analysis). With today's modes of communication and the related technologies, an almost complete coverage of all organisational communication is within reach. Email, chats and collaboration software are state of the art, almost all telephone calls are run through unified messaging systems and video conferencing has become a standard form of interaction even locally these days. Add in real-time translation and transcription (speech to text) and we have a nearly complete coverage of all formal and of most informal communication. Machine learning with its natural language processing (NLP) techniques provides the tools to extract topics, content and meaning from all communication and also to find out relations between individual documents and communication streams. All this would allow us to move from int´formation flow analysis to content flow analysis. It would be possible to follow the flow of the content, the meaning and even the feelings and emotions through the organisation. We would not just look at communication bottlenecks and shortcuts but also on sources of information and sinks and could even see where relevant filters are and how they work or identify sources and types of noise harming the efficiency of communication.

While today, all this is technically possible, a word of caution needs to be added here: for the quantitative analyses, we could relatively easily anonymise the data to comply with the applicable rules for data protection and privacy. This is much more difficult to achieve for the content flow analysis, as anonymised global contents could neutralise much of the crucial information. (While I already called the use of structural information a nightmare for any data protection officer, using communication data to analyse the flow of content might feel like being in hell for him or her.) Using all the information from content flow analysis might be not a big deal in the realms of intelligence agencies, in a corporate world it will be extremely difficult to find a mode under which we could run a full-fledged analysis.

Solutions

Having read and hopefully understood in the previous chapters a lot about elements, functions, and their respective shortcomings, one might ask, what solutions can be derived from such knowledge. Before looking at the answers and possible solutions, let us look at the question first. What is it that needs to be optimised? As we have seen above, for most organisations, the flow of information is their only connection to the outside world. The nodes of the organisational network, the employees, its members, etc. are what makes up an organisation – and those nodes are the limiting factor of how much a network can do. There is no way of increasing the maximum processing capacity of any person individually.

To serve their purpose, organisations need to take up information from their environment, process it, and send it back to be turned into actions that foster the organisation's purpose (money, health, entertainment, a better world...). Essentially, what we need to improve is the pathway:

perception →information in →process →information out →action

or in other words, we need to optimise the communication of the organisation with its environment within a constrained setting.

While communication is often touted as being essential to modern organisations and a whole industry is busying itself working on inter- and intra-company communication solutions, the answer to the question above is less evident than it might seem. As we have seen before, an organisation only can generate value or serve its purpose when it sends information across its boundaries that induce actions at the receiving end. This is the communication that is key, i.e. without it, an organisation would not make much sense. Information that is sent and received within the organisation, on the other hand, does not immediately generate value or serve the organisation's purpose. It is merely bridging the gaps that have been created by sharing the organisations' work among the members of the organisation. Ideally, as shown above, the whole organisation acts as one node with a single brain and thus does not require any internal communication while being as efficient as possible.

From this viewpoint, all internal communication must be viewed as waste – waste of cognitive resources – rather than being key. Whatever resources are spent on communication are taken away from thinking, innovating, and supporting the value generation. After all human cognitive capacity is the primary resource of an organisation (probably the only resource that most organisations can draw upon) and is limited to 20-30 bits/s. Rather than maximising communication, the task is to organise communication in a way that leaves room for ideas and innovation while ensuring that the required administrative and structural information, as well as information to induce knowledge, reaches the right nodes.

In other words, the optimisation target is efficiency of the organisation. We can approach this from three ends:

- Use the bandwidth of the information channels more efficient

- Avoid losses in the cognitive information processing at the node level

- Adjust the network structure to make information flow better

- Ensure that only purposeful information is flowing through the network

8.1 Efficient use of channels

The capacities and bandwidths discussed previously are just describing the theoretical capacity level/limit. In reality, human communication is imperfect, human thinking is imperfect. All this reduces the actual available capacity far below the theoretical level. To counteract, we need to understand where and how those losses are occurring – the effectiveness can be increased only by changing how people communicate with each other, reduce misunderstanding, push back fallacies, improve the density of information, motivation, understanding, common goals, etc. The Bandwidth of the available channels and cognitive resources needs to be shared between all communication requirements:

- Communication serving the *purpose of the organisation*, this is the communication that is the core of the organisation's reason for being, the central flow of information from the environment back into the environment.

- *organisational or structural information* that is required to be channelled to the individual nodes to ensure they know their task and position in the network, the more dynamic the organisation is, the larger the respective load is.

- *Knowledge transfer* that is required to ensure that all nodes have the capabilities to do what they are supposed to and to maintain such a state. A more dynamic environment and constant changes will require more information flow to ensure all nodes' capabilities are up to their changing tasks.

- *World model information*, such as vision, culture or strategy needs to be transported to all nodes and incorporated into their world model

- *Emotions, feelings*, etc. will also be shared through the same channels to foster trustful relationships and credibility

All these communication and processing needs need to be fulfilled by the available bandwidth. The bandwidth that each communication need requires will change over time and also depend on the dynamics of the organisation and the environment. However, the way an organisation steers the sequence of the flow will have an impact on how the overall information flow develops in the future. As we have seen above, whatever we perceive and think, depends on what model of the world we base it on. The better the state of such a model, the better and more efficient and purposeful (especially regarding the purpose of the organisation) the information will be processed. This includes simple things such as the alignment on concepts or even the definition of words and meanings, we easily can talk at cross purposes for quite a while until we realise that we apply different meanings to same words. The more obvious a definition appears to us, the more emphasis we need to put on ensuring that our peer understands it the same way. Therefore, putting emphasis on building up such a model, put down definitions and concepts, will avoid misunderstanding, errors, and inferior output later on. Therefore, teaching the required capabilities and vision, culture, and strategy early on is absolutely useful to have a more precise and efficient communication later. Besides, even with a finely tuned sequence

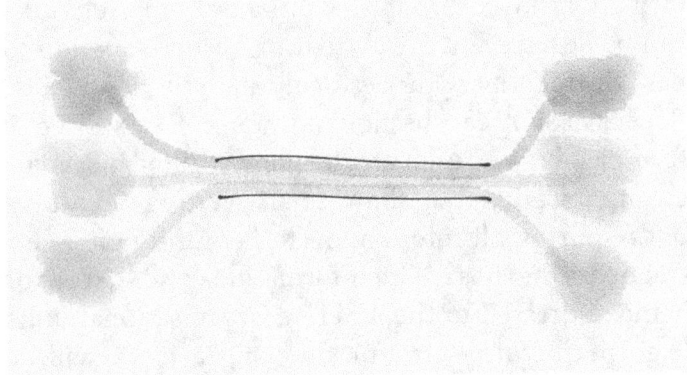

of transporting information through the networks, there will be much noise and unnecessary information blocking the channels. Consequently, we need to work on avoiding ambiguous information, half-baked knowledge or erroneous data being sent through the network, as each communication of semi-useful information will trigger a tedious question and answer sequence eating up a lot of bandwidth. Some of the efficiency can be introduced by proper training and teaching, as described above. Working on the quality of data and their immediate availability will also contribute to significantly lower usage of the bandwidth.

8.2 Network architecture

While the efficiency of the individual communication pathways is one step to improving the organisational efficiency, the structure of an organisational network plays a no less important part in how well information flows through an organisation. Networks can be designed in a way that makes information to pass through many nodes or through numerous bottlenecks, or it can be flowing more or less directly from sender to receiver. Imagine a fully hierarchical organisation, not allowing any cutting of corners but requiring all information to flow through a central node, the 'boss' – all information coming from or being addressed to the different organisational units (e.g. marketing, sales, production, it, etc.) will be limited down to 20-30 bits/s (or even less if there is some thinking involved). The closer it gets to the central node, the more it needs to be stripped down to the essential ('essential' being defined by the world model of hierarchy doing so). It then flows back down the hierarchy of another part of the organisation, eventually being enriched with information (coming from the world model of the respective hierarchy). With such an extreme example, it becomes clear that the structure of the organisation and the communication networks plays a vital role in the efficiency of the communication of an organisation. The intra-organisational network needs to be designed in a way that minimises the amount of information that is transported within the organisation. This can be done by reducing the network distance between the communication parties, by eliminating circular communication, by not separating the decision-makers from the knowledge holders (e.g. move the decision power down to the ones being closest to the knowledge) or by installing pathways to shorten the flows, e.g. by strengthening informal networks and communities of experts. To organise teams in a way that requires only little steering and structural training will reduce the amount of structural and organisational information that has to be sent through the network. Instead of setting up teams with members of each participating sub-organisation (and having to report back often) – set up teams just by bringing in the required resources capabilities and let them organise and delineate responsibilities between themselves. The amount of communication required for organisational and structural information would be reduced and only flowing directly between the team members. Design your organisational setup by following the actual flow of the information. If an org-chart is only describing the information flow for 'A reports to B' and 'B supervises A' while all other information takes other pathways, that organisational structure is probably not really essential to the functioning of an organisation, but instead takes away bandwidth from where it is needed. Furthermore, try to employ people only where human ingenuity and interpersonal skills are needed. All repetitive work can probably be automated to a large extent. See also 8.4 "Technology" further below. Avoid working modes that create a lot of organisational communication. Multitasking and asynchronous work, as we have seen, result in an increase in non-purposeful information flow (following up, managing time slots, prioritisation efforts, etc.) Make knowledge available to the ones needing it, fight fragmented knowledge. Simply transporting information from one end of the network to the other is just wasting bandwidth. Make sure that the people who need to know can acquire the relevant information, assemble teams based on the required knowledge and use proper technology the support availability of information. In short, design your organisation alongside the flow of information and not against it.

8.3 Mudas

Taking a different view and borrowing from the world of automotive production systems, we can optimise the organisational efficiency by reducing the waste, the so-called mudas (Japanese for futility; uselessness; wastefulness). The concept of eliminating waste is "is the key to efficiency – in the Toyota Production System, this is termed as Muda, Muri, and Mura. [...] Muda means waste and refers in management terms to a wide range of non-value-adding activities. Eliminating waste is one of the main principles of the Just-in-time system, the main pillar of the Toyota Production System. Considered as waste are unnecessary financing costs, storage costs, worthless stock of old items etc. Muda of overproduction and Muda of Inventory are the most common ones." [65] Muri (overburden) is what already Weaver mentioned when speaking about the effects of overloading channels[62]: " *[...] that error and confusion arise and fidelity decreases, when, no matter how good the coding, one tries to crowd too much over a channel".*

Mura (unevenness/irregularity) one could also relate to an uneven cognitive workload or lousy timing (waiting for important matters until the very last minute, so they suddenly become urgent and push a more ordered communication aside. However, let us focus on the mudas now. Adapting the production mudas to communication, we get the following 7 primary sources of waste in organisational communication (see also [34][6]):

- *Transport*: moving information between people to get a decision, complete a task, etc.

- *Inventory*: generating and maintaining and storing information beyond its need

- *Motion*: unnecessary changes in the environment (organisation, goals, working mode)

- *Waiting*: wait for others to provide information

so you can complete a task

- *Over-processing* – involving more people and steps than needed, non-value-adding activities

- *Defects*: wrong information, incorrect or ambiguous information (low Data quality)

- *Over-production*:creating more detail and content than was asked for

All those wastes relate to information that has been or will be transported through the network without being necessary and creating value in the end like also discussed in 8.2 "Efficient use of channels". They crowd the information channels and cognitive capacities in the network and prevent us from doing something valuable instead.

8.4 Technology

Where does modern communication technology come in? Where should we put the human resources, where should we establish automation? To date, creativity is the exclusive domain of human brains in the organisational context. Modern artificial intelligence yet has to prove that it can be creative – albeit depending on the definition of creativity being used. The best we can currently have is algorithms that build on past experiences and human expertise and make predictions that sometimes can be extending to related fields. For recurring tasks, rule-based processing of information and providing access to information, information technology systems are the best choice. We should not assign mere mailbox tasks to people or even use people to carry information from one system to the other.

Using the metaphor of a sphere of the 'known' in the universe of the 'unknown' (cave – this is not the inside/outside world depiction from above), organisations are typically trying to increase the sphere of the *'known'* by exploring the *'unknown'* at its borders and turning it into the *'known'* (or connect to other spheres floating around in the universe of the unknown, e.g. by buying knowledge or whole companies). While the established, structured knowledge is located in the core of the sphere, the further we move towards the border to the unknown, the less established and structured and linked the knowledge becomes.

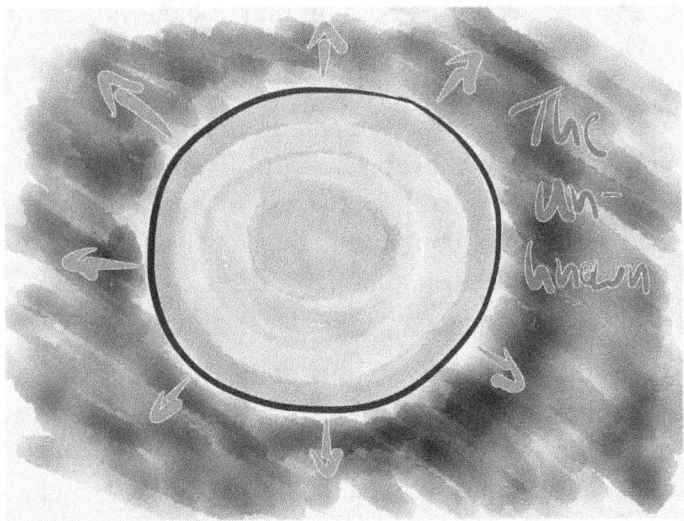

Here, the scarce resources of the human brains should be placed as far from the centre as possible – with the structured, well-known areas in the being covered by automation. Human brains are good at sense-making, they continuously are scanning the world around them, or at least the information flowing in and try to match it to their model of the world. Unexpected information leads to dissonances and then eventually to the adjustment of the world model once those dissonances have been confirmed to be real. In the context of an organisation, human brains can do precisely that perfectly at the border between the ‚known‘ and the ‚unknown‘. This is a zone where innovation is happening, bringing the ‘adjacent possible’ [31] to life. Computer systems are good at holding information, rule-based processing and are almost agnostic to the amount of information flowing through them (just buy more processor capacity). So, adding them to a communication network provides you with highly connected nodes – every user represents a connection – with unlimited communication capacity when compared to brains. They just lack cognitive capacity. The design of the rules they follow and the quality of the information being input determines the quality of the output. Even modern artificial intelligence still applies algorithms, albeit very complex ones, to compute their results, they still lack any kind of intentional or associative capabilities.

Today, in a world where the problem is the abundance of information rather than its scarcity, like in past times, the task of finding what you need in all the information that you have has become the real challenge. (see also [13]) This is where computer systems are of increasing help. Support for searching, pre-processing, condensing – always based on what we tell them upfront -has become the hot field of information system application. So here you have nodes that can perform part of the consolidation of information for you and have the capability and capacity of doing this for all the information that ever circulated through your organisation. (This is not to speak of organisations using physical and cyber-physical systems generating data at the rate of megabits per second that require different approaches).

'Digital'as an end in itself won't do much good for an organisation. Only if it is used as a means to the end called 'communication and information processing', it can help you solve issues preventing you from communicating efficiently, e.g. by enhancing the information content and density, or by consolidating fragmented information, or even by helping to organise collaboration in a better way, etc. So, make your analysis of what is not working well in your organisation. If you need tools, then look for tools re-

solving just that, a state of the art knowledge management systems, a new communication platform etc.
Just going 'digital' with all other pieces remaining un-
changed will not get you too far, though. It is important to understand that just implementing a great
system and not changing the processes and the way
the people in your organisation work will not bring
success. With the way you manage knowledge and
information and communication, also your organisation should be adapted. [8]

8.4.1 Shorten pathways

Technology can support communication by shorten-
ing the pathways. In a global organisation, people
working together on one topic or project are often
separated spatially – they may sit in a different city,
country, or continent. Technology already has a
tremendous share in the way that global organisations work – even that they can act globally at all.
In the same manner, technology can bridge organisational gaps, connect virtual teams by putting them
into their own virtual workspaces with whiteboards,
chats, and file storage. Last but not least, we also have
gaps in time. While phone calls, video-conferences,
or in-person meetings are enabling people to synchronously communicate, chats, email and messen-
gers allow people to communicate synchronously or
asynchronously and seamlessly change between the
modes. Shorter pathways mean fewer nodes have to
relay information and reduce traffic in the network.

As each node on the network runs the information through its filters, each edge introducing noise, having fewer hops between nodes also reduces the error rate and the speed at which information reaches the receiver. All this leaves more room for other, more purposeful information processing and innovation

8.4.2 Pre-digest data

Another vital role that technology can and should play is to pre-digest the information that pours into an organisation. While during much of the time people lived in a state of information scarcity -- partially because the ones running the kingdom or the state feared well-informed citizens, partially because distributing information was determined how much stories a person could remember or how much paper she could carry and how fast and far he could travel – we are now living in the state of having much more information at our fingertips than we need or that we ever can take up. Consequently, today's' task is to find the piece of information in the massive haystack of information that is available to us. This is precisely what search engines, artificial intelligence and language processing, and many other modern tools are made for. If we put them to use in a perfect manner, the organisation will just receive the amount of information that it needs and can process.

I should add a word of caution. Any pre-digesting,

compressing, and selecting of information is similar to our brain's filters that are tasked to make a similar reduction of information, and come with lots of potential malfunctions, fallacies, closed-loop steered perception, etc. It might be a good idea to install some mechanism that allows the organisation to bypass those filters from time to time and re-adjust their bearing.

8.4.3 Information storage and retrieval

What our brain calls remembering is a role that we have invented knowledge management systems for. The process of knowledge management is "a conscious strategy of getting the right knowledge to the right people at the right time and helping people share and put information into action in ways that strive to improve organisational performance" [51]. While there are numerous similar and differing definitions available, this statement beautifully highlights that knowledge management tries to achieve for an organisation what we take as a given function of our brain. Ideally, KM delivers the information you need, when you need it, no matter where it usually would reside, eliminating all the deficiencies stemming from communication deficits, from forgetting, from information overload. It puts all the information into one place, removing the need to know someone who knows someone who knows what you need to complete your task. In the communication network, knowledge management systems would represent a very central, densely connected node that everyone can access immediately, the bandwidth only limited by the speed of understanding at the receivers' end. It would free an enormous bandwidth for creativity, flexibility, and innovation – and probably remove a good number of nodes (people), too, all the ones acting as brokers of information and gate-keepers.

8.5 Human-System interaction

While systems are generally designed to be solutions to information processing challenges, they are typically designed for a particular, known 'problem space' only. (When we speak of systems today we usually refer to computerised systems, but systems can also exist outside of the domain of computer technology.) Systems usually are used to connect people within an organisation or across organisational borders. Systems may 'speak' to each other, too, in the end, there will always be some human on the sending and receiving side in the long run. (We may in the future see computer systems than never communicate to humans, but then they are useless to us humans or vice versa.) Systems tragically also are susceptible to the effects of growth and complexity that also affect organisations. As reality never matches the assumed reality at the point of systems design, systems often do not work extremely well, or as John Gall put it pointedly: "Systems in general work poorly or not at all" [23]. This is probably an extreme statement, systems mostly do exactly what they were designed for, process and communicate information, in the form of workflows or databases to be queried – exactly just that. We must nevertheless acknowledge that the above-mentioned gaps between the domain that the systems were designed for and reality exists and needs to be closed. Bridging these gaps, coping with unforeseen complexity is where humans need to come in to make the whole setup work. A huge number of jobs are created around every system that is coming to life – administration and maintenance, development, bug-fixing, help desks, people working on the interfaces between systems, people training other people on the use of the systems, service technicians and finally the users themselves who are the connections between the systems and the organisation. While only the users and the system itself will transport and process purposeful information, all the other efforts are secondary. They need to considered as waste in the sense of organisational efficiency (the global equivalent to this effect is the growth of what David Graeber coined as 'bullshit jobs', to describe jobs that exist only because also on a global level, systems are not working very well. [14]) From the point of organisational communication, therefore, we need to be very careful about how we design or processes and how we automate them.

Summary

Organisations consist of people, and people have brains. There are no organisations without communication – communication is a prerequisite for calling a group of people an 'organisation'. Organisations influence their environment to serve their purpose – which can be making money, achieving a specific goal, changing the world, etc. Organisations attain this by mainly focusing on processing and transforming information into decisions and actions. The efficiency of an organisation is determined by the result of those actions it can induce (such as the amount of money that was earned, by how much the world became a better place, etc.). Internal processing of information can only be a means, not an end to the organisation's purpose and cannot create any immediate value.

Human brains are made for communication. Human brains are made to ensure the proliferation of humankind. Consequently, we only perceive what we need to perceive to survive and proliferate. Our cognitive capacity is somewhat limited, our senses a bit less. We only can perceive a tiny part of the world through the signals our senses pick up. There is a huge surge of information flowing in through our eyes, ears and all other senses. Our brains need to drastically reduce that information rate to a level that we can handle cognitively, hoping that nothing important gets lost. We employ filters and shortcuts to do this. Those filters and shortcuts are influenced by what we expect and predict. What we expect and predict is governed mainly by what model of the world we maintain within our brain. This model is what we actually live in, not the world around us.

An organisation is bound and limited by the capabilities of its individual nodes – the brains of the people that are making up the organisation. To drive an organisation to function in an optimal way, we need to consider those capabilities and design it in a way that lets the relevant, purposeful information flow in the best possible way. Our cognitive capacities are an often neglected but crucial design parameter for the setup of an organisation. Only nodes interacting with the world outside of the organisation can create immediate value. All other nodes only can support the value generation. Consequently, when setting up an organisation, designing processes or assigning tasks, we need to ensure that the interaction with the environment is maximised and secondary tasks are limited to what is necessary.

Many effects reduce the theoretically best possible way of working of an organisation down to a fraction of what could be. Unnecessary communication, redundancy, half baked knowledge, structure, working style, lack of training, a different understanding of the goals, the functioning of the organisation and the world around it, time constraints – all interact with one another in a self-amplifying manner. An organisational structure that is not well-designed leads to the effect of structural and organisational information flows clogging the pathways, crowding out the

purposeful information. Typically that is then coun-
tered by putting more effort into prioritisation and
firefighting, taking away even more cognitive capacities that should be used for purposeful work. Increasing the pressure will lead to people cutting down
on their flexibility, which requires even more coordination and so on. All this is driving down the efficiency of the organisation in a vicious downward
spiral. Optimising the efficiency of an organisation,
after all, does not mean that the people forming it
will be exploited to a maximum, instead, it means
that everybody can have the best possible contribu-
tion to the purpose of the organisation, which should,
after all, be the main reason of being there in the first
place. Instead, we need to think an organisation

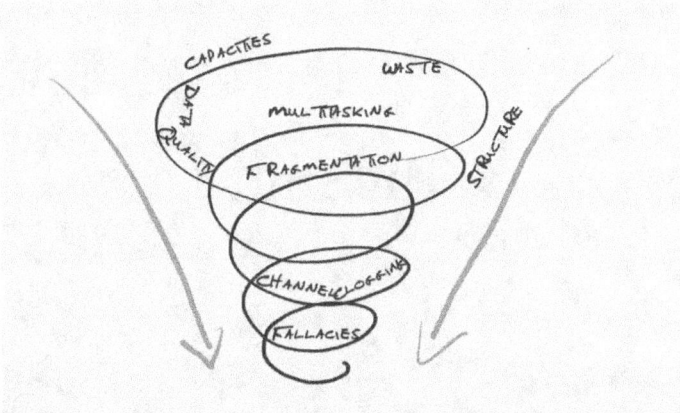

from the perspective of the communication that is required to foster its purpose, be it value or the well-
being of mankind. Understand what the organisation
is existing for, define the required interaction with
the world and design the information flow in a manner that keeps you in a stable cycle, avoiding being

dragged down into the self-sustaining bureaucracy. Focus on the purposeful communication and restrict and reduce all the other communication as it is taking away capacity. Only the purposeful communication is key, all other communication is waste!

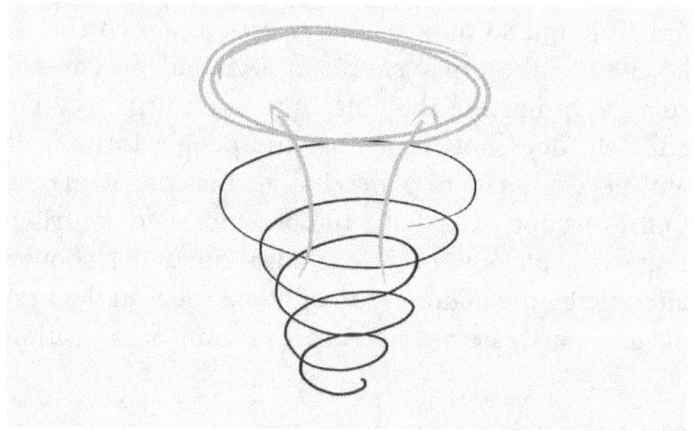

The End

Recommended Reading

The following books are a selection of all the
literature I read and consulted for ideas, concepts
and information. They provided much of what forms
the backbone of the overview that I introduced on
the previous pages. If you need some ideas on books
to read, please have a look at the following list
(sorted by the last names of authors, not importance
or intellectual depth):

The human nottleneck, Richard Epworth [20]
The case against reality, Donald Hoffman [27]
Where good ideas come from, Steven Johnson [31]
Thinking, fast and slow, Daniel Kahnemann [32]
Scale, Geoffrey West[70]
Also, I would like to mention the *Systems Bible* by
John Gall [23] in which he pokes in a humorous
manner into the many shortfalls of modern
organisations and systems.

The Author

I was born in Hamburg, Germany in the late sixties and consequently now are in my early fifties, living in a small town in Germany. I am an engineer by training and by heart with a PhD in Biotechnology. After a short stay in biotechnology research I joined a multinational company working out of Germany. While I spent my initial years working as an engineer or close to that, I found myself slowly but steadily moving from the physical world to a world that saw me spend more and more of my day in trading information with internal and external partners — a classical corporate office job . What is now many years of experience in such a global and corporate environment, gaining some insight into the workings of such organisations, made me wonder how things work and why they work despite all the shortcomings that I inevitably learned about. Regularly, I found myself sitting with colleagues Over lunch, with partners from other companies at dinner or friends from other environments musing over systems, organisations and how they communicate. Spending some time in the bookshops of airports and train stations got me interested in books on small and large systems, psychology, the brain, economics and so on - all about systems and interactions of some kind. From time to time, I am also working as an assistant lecturer at a nearby university trying to explain the world of manufacturing data to students.

All the other hours of the days I am a grandfather, father and husband (and like to tinker a bit or tend my flowers, fruits and vegetables). I have never written anything complex since my theses during my university days until setting out to write about how us humans perform and communicate in organisational settings. I hope I won't disappoint my prospective readers though.

Acknowledgements

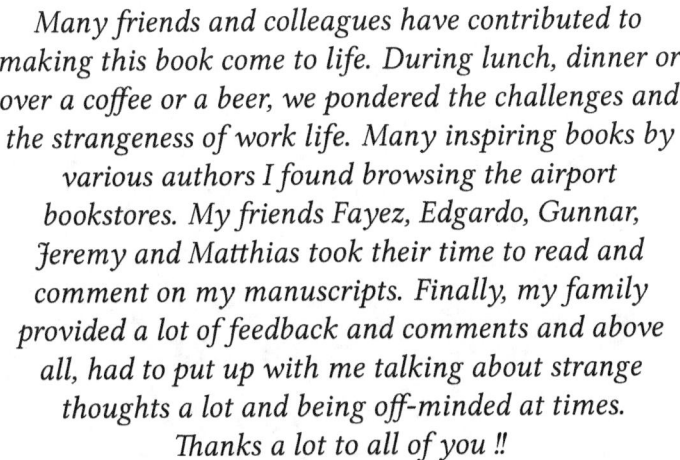

Many friends and colleagues have contributed to making this book come to life. During lunch, dinner or over a coffee or a beer, we pondered the challenges and the strangeness of work life. Many inspiring books by various authors I found browsing the airport bookstores. My friends Fayez, Edgardo, Gunnar, Jeremy and Matthias took their time to read and comment on my manuscripts. Finally, my family provided a lot of feedback and comments and above all, had to put up with me talking about strange thoughts a lot and being off-minded at times. Thanks a lot to all of you !!

Special credits go to all the people providing templates, resources, programs and advice providing the technology and knowledge for my publishing process. Particular thoughts go out to all the authors of the wonderful and inspiring books that inspired me to assemble my model of the world or organisational communication, all the scientists publishing those papers helping me to bridge many of the gaps that I encountered during my journey.

Ulrich

The Book's Story

I never meant to write a book. It came about without my knowing. Following numerous discussions about the strangeness of work-life among friends and colleagues, it started with a mind-map trying to give some order to those thoughts. Then I went on to sketch what I had in mind. When I realised that many of the books I loved to buy in airport bookstores were providing valuable background to my observations, I went into active research mode. The internet is an endless and valuable source for publications on any subject that one can think of. It allowed me to explore more details of various aspects and thoughts and to fill much of the white space. Suddenly I had a small document in my hands that was attempting to connect all the bits and pieces. With an abundance of information and ideas at hand, the main problem became to stop reading and searching. Consequently, my texts grew, and I passed the point of no return. What was I going to do with a heap of conceptual fragments, sketches and drawings? Now - here's a book, small, but my honest attempt to externalise my thoughts. I hope you like it. If you are missing something or feel the need to cast doubts on some of my reasonings, please let me know – by adding comments in the online shop where you bought the book, or by sending me an email. You'll find the relevant channels in the publishers section at the beginning of the book. I'll try to read and answer to the extent possible, within my 30 bits/s

Bibliography

[1]   R. L. Ackoff. "From Data to Wisdom." In: *Journal of Applied Systems Analysis* 16 (1989).

[2]   Daniel L. Ames et al. "Contextual alignment of cognitive and neural dynamics." In: *Journal of cognitive neuroscience* 27.4 (2015), pp. 655–664. DOI: 10.1162/jocn{\textunderscore}a{\textunderscore}00728.

[3]   Benjamin C. Ampel, Mark Muraven, and Ewan C. McNay. "Mental Work Requires Physical Energy: Self-Control Is Neither Exception nor Exceptional." In: *Frontiers in psychology* 9 (2018), p. 1005. ISSN: 1664-1078. DOI: 10.3389/fpsyg.2018.01005.

[4]   APA Dictionary of Psychology. *Trust - definition.* 2020. URL: https://dictionary.apa.org/trust.

[5]   Paul Atchley. *You Can't Multitask, So Stop Trying.* Ed. by Harvard Business Review. 2010. URL: https://hbr.org/2010/12/you-cant-multi-task-so-stop-tr.

[6]   Bahman Jamshidi Eini et al. "MUDA IN THE TELECOMMUNICATION AND INFORMATION INFRASTRUCTURE OF THE SMART GRID." In: (2014). URL: https://www.semanticscholar.org/paper/MUDA-IN-THE-TELECOMMUNICATION-AND-INFORMATION-OF-Eini-Kamran/8b98e612dcfde0ea6d5e3e6e3bc84ee398b8643b.

[7]   R. F. Baumeister et al. "Ego depletion: is the active self a limited resource?" In: *Journal of personality and social psychology* 74.5 (1998), pp. 1252–1265. ISSN: 0022-3514. DOI: 10.1037//0022-3514.74.5.1252.

[8]   Irma Becerra-Fernandez, D. E. Leidner, and Dorothy Leidner, eds. *Knowledge Management: An Evolutionary View: The Impact of Computer-Mediated Communication on Knowledge Transfer.* 2nd ed. Hoboken: Taylor and Francis, 2014. ISBN: 978-0-7656-1637-1. URL: http://gbv.eblib.com/patron/FullRecord.aspx?p=1900092.

[9]   F. Behr et al. "Estimating and comparing entropies across written natural languages using PPM compression." In: *2003 Data Compression Conference.* Los Alamitos and Piscataway: IEEE Computer Society Press, Jan. 2003, p. 416. ISBN: 0-7695-1896-6. DOI: 10.1109/DCC.2003.1194035.

[10]   Buster Benson. "Cognitive bias cheat sheet, simplified - Why Are We Yelling? - Medium." In: *Why Are We Yelling?* (8.1.2017). URL: https://medium.com/thinking-is-hard/4-conundrums-of-intelligence-2ab78d90740f.

[11]   Cambridge Dictionary Online. *NETWORK | meaning in the Cambridge English Dictionary.* 29.3.2020. URL: https://dictionary.cambridge.org/dictionary/english/network.

[12]   Christopher Chabris and Daniel Simons. *The Invisible Gorilla: And Other Ways Our Intuitions Deceive Us.* Ed. by Christopher Chabris and Daniel Simons. 2010. URL: http://www.theinvisiblegorilla.com/gorilla_experiment.html.

[13]   Kenneth Cukier. *The data deluge.* 2020-05-03T19:16:17.000Z. URL: https://www.economist.com/leaders/2010/02/25/the-data-deluge.

[14]   David Graeber. *On the Phenomenon of Bullshit Jobs: A Work Rant.* 2013. URL: https://www.strike.coop/bullshit-jobs/.

[15]   T. Dávid-Barrett and R. I. M. Dunbar. "Processing power limits social group size: computational evidence for the cognitive costs of sociality." In: *Proceedings. Biological sciences* 280.1765 (2013), p. 20131151. DOI: 10.1098/rspb.2013.1151.

[16]   Guy Deutscher. *Through the language glass: Why the world looks different in other languages.* London: Arrow Books, 2011. ISBN: 9780099505570.

[17]   Rolf Dobelli. *The art of thinking clearly.* 2014. ISBN: 1444794876.

[18]   R. I. M. Dunbar. "The social brain hypothesis and its implications for social evolution." In: *Annals of human biology* 36.5 (2009), pp. 562–572. DOI: 10.1080/03014460902960289.

[19]   Michelle Effros. *Shannon's Channel and Capacity.* 2016. URL: https://www.youtube.com/watch?v=t_AYln-O2_o.

[20]   Richard Epworth. *Bottleneck - Our Human Interface with Reality: The Our Human Interface with Reality: The Disturbing and Exciting Implications of its True Nature: Bottleneck - Our Human Interface with Reality: The Disturbing and Exciting Implications of its True Nature.* 2014.

[21]   Richard Epworth. *The difference between sensing and experience.* June 28, 2015. URL: http://www.humanbottleneck.com/blog/page/2/.

[22]   Matthew T. Gailliot and Roy F. Baumeister. "The physiology of willpower: linking blood glucose to self-control." In: *Personality and social psychology review : an official journal of the Society for Personality and Social Psychology, Inc* 11.4 (2007), pp. 303–327. ISSN: 1088-8683. DOI: 10.1177/1088868307303030.

[23]   John Gall. *The systems bible: The beginner's guide to systems large and small : being the third edition of Systemantics.* Third Edition, Fifth printing. Walker, Minnesota: General Systemantics Press, 2014. ISBN: 0-9618251-7-0.

[24]   Clive Gamble, John Gowlett, and Robin I. M. Dunbar. *Thinking big: How the evolution of social life shaped the human mind.* London: Thames & Hudson, 2014. ISBN: 9780500051801.

[25]   Thomas E. Harris and Mark D. Nelson. *Applied organizational communication: Theory and practice in a global environment.* 3. ed. LEA's communication series. New York, NY: Erlbaum, 2008. ISBN: 9780805859409.

[26]   Uri Hasson. "This is your brain on communication." In: *ideas.ted.com* (27.1.2017). URL: https://ideas.ted.com/this-is-your-brain-on-communication/.

[27]   Donald D. Hoffman. *The case against reality: Why evolution hid the truth from our eyes.* First edition. New York: W.W. Norton & Company, 2019. ISBN: 0393254690.

[28] Donald D. Hoffman, Manish Singh, and Chetan Prakash. "The Interface Theory of Perception." In: *Psychonomic bulletin & review* 22.6 (2015), pp. 1480–1506. DOI: 10.3758/s13423-015-0890-8.

[29] H. Jeong et al. "The large-scale organization of metabolic networks." In: *Nature* 407.6804 (2000), pp. 651–654. ISSN: 0028-0836. DOI: 10.1038/35036627.

[30] John Tierney. *Do You Suffer From Decision Fatigue?* Ed. by The New York Times. 7.3.2020. URL: https://www.nytimes.com/2011/08/21/magazine/do-you-suffer-from-decision-fatigue.html?pagewanted=all.

[31] Steven Johnson. *Where good ideas come from: The natural history of innovation.* New York: Riverhead Books, 2010. ISBN: 9781594487712.

[32] Daniel Kahneman. *Thinking, fast and slow.* London: Penguin Books, 2012. ISBN: 9780141033570.

[33] Michael Kalloniatis and Charles Luu, eds. *Webvision: The Organization of the Retina and Visual System [Internet].* University of Utah Health Sciences Center, 2007.

[34] Faddoul Khoukhi, Mohamed Bahaj, and Mostafa Ezziyyani, eds. *Smart Data and Computational Intelligence: Proceedings of the International Conference on Advanced Information Technology, Services and Systems (AIT2S-18) Held on October 17 - 18, 2018 in Mohammedia.* Vol. 66. Lecture Notes in Networks and Systems. Cham: Springer International Publishing, 2019. ISBN: 978-3-030-11913-3. DOI: 10.1007/978-3-030-11914-0. URL: http://dx.doi.org/10.1007/978-3-030-11914-0.

[35] Jefferey Kluger. *Why You're Pretty Much Unconscious All the Time.* Ed. by time magazine. 2015. URL: https://time.com/3937351/consciousness-unconsciousness-brain/.

[36] A. N. Kolmogorov. "Three approaches to the quantitative definition of information *." In: *International Journal of Computer Mathematics* 2.1-4 (1968), pp. 157–168. ISSN: 0020-7160. DOI: 10.1080/00207166808803030.

[37] Martin Korte. *Wir sind Gedächtnis: Wie unsere Erinnerungen bestimmen, wer wir sind.* 1. Auflage. München: Deutsche Verlags-Anstalt, 2017. ISBN: 9783641163181.

[38] David Krackhardt and Jeffrey R. Hanson. *Informal Networks: The Company Behind the Chart.* 1993. URL: https://hbr.org/1993/07/informal-networks-the-company-behind-the-chart (visited on).

[39] Arthur D. Lander. "How cells know where they are." In: *Science (New York, N.Y.)* 339.6122 (2013), pp. 923–927. DOI: 10.1126/science.1224186.

[40] Steen Larsen. "Information can be Transmitted but Knowledge must be Induced." In: *PLET: Programmed Learning & Educational Technology* 23.4 (1986), pp. 331–336. ISSN: 0951-0907. DOI: 10.1080/0033039860230403.

[41] Jessica Leber. "The Immortal Life of the Enron E-mails." In: *MIT Technology Review* (2.7.2013). URL: https://www.technologyreview.com/2013/07/02/177506/the-immortal-life-of-the-enron-e-mails/.

[42]   lexico.com. *Decision | Meaning of Decision by Lexico*. 16.4.2020. URL: https:
        //www.lexico.com/definition/decision.

[43]   Ning Lu and Xuemin Shen. *Capacity analysis of vehicular communication
        networks*. Springer-briefs in electrical and computer engineering. New
        York, NY: Springer, 2014. ISBN: 9781461483977.

[44]   Karl Marx, Johannes Rohbeck, and Peggy H. Breitenstein, eds.
        Philosophische und ökonomische Schriften. Vol. 18554. Reclams Universal-
        Bibliothek. Stuttgart: Reclam, 2008. ISBN: 9783150185544.

[45]   merriam-webster.com. *Definition of MEANING*. 2.4.2020. URL: https://
        www.merriam-webster.com/dictionary/meaning.

[46]   Andreas Molitor. *Hausgemachte Verwirrung - brand eins online*. Ed. by
        BrandEins. 9.3.2020. URL: https : / / www . brandeins . de / magazine /
        brand - eins - wirtschaftsmagazin / 2019 / komplexitaet / hausgemachte -
        verwirrung.

[47]   Ezequiel Morsella et al. "Homing in on consciousness in the nervous
        system: An action-based synthesis." In: *The Behavioral and brain sciences*
        39 (2016), e168. DOI: 10.1017/S0140525X15000643.

[48]   C. Girija Navaneedhan and T. J. Kamalanabhan. "What Is Meant by Cog-
        nitive Structures? How Does It Influence Teaching –Learning of Psychol-
        ogy?" In: *IRA International Journal of Education and Multidisciplinary
        Studies (ISSN 2455-2526)* 7.2 (2017), p. 89. DOI: 10.21013/jems.v7.n2.p5.

[49]   Chris Nodder. *Evil by Design: Interaction design to lead us into tempta-
        tion*. Hoboken: Wiley, 2013. ISBN: 9781118422144. URL: http://search.
        ebscohost.com/login.aspx?direct=true&scope=site&db=nlebk&db=
        nlabk&AN=588874.

[50]   nzherald. *Maps without New Zealand: The worst offenders revealed*. 2018.

[51]   Carla O'Dell and C. Jackson Grayson. "If Only We Knew What We Know:
        Identification and Transfer of Internal Best Practices." In: *California Man-
        agement Review* 40.3 (1998), pp. 154–174. ISSN: 0008-1256. DOI: 10.2307/
        41165948. URL: http://www.iiakm.org/ojakm/articles/2015/volume3_1/
        OJAKM_Volume3_1pp1-20.pdf.

[52]   OSS. *1944 OSS Simple Sabotage Field Manual*. OSS, 1944. URL: https://gist.
        github.com/kennwhite/467529962c184258d08f16daec83d5da.

[53]   Brandon Oto. "When thinking is hard: managing decision fatigue..." In:
        EMS World 41 (2012).

[54]   Parkinsons law. *Parkinson's law*. Ed. by Wikipedia. n.d. URL: https://en.
        wikipedia.org/w/index.php?title=Parkinson's_law&oldid=961042457.

[55]   A. K. Pati and S. L. Braunstein. "Impossibility of deleting an unknown
        quantum state." In: *Nature* 404.6774 (2000), pp. 164–165. ISSN: 0028-0836.
        DOI: 10.1038/35004532.

[56]   François Pellegrino, Christophe Coupé, and Egidio Marsico. "Across-
        Language Perspective on Speech Information Rate." In: *Language* 87.3
        (2011), pp. 539–558. ISSN: 1535-0665. DOI: 10.1353/lan.2011.0057. URL:
        https://muse.jhu.edu/article/449938/pdf.

[57] Dimitris A. Pinotsis, Timothy J. Buschman, and Earl K. Miller. "Working Memory Load Modulates Neuronal Coupling." In: *Cerebral cortex (New York, N.Y. : 1991)* 29.4 (2019), pp. 1670–1681. DOI: 10.1093/cercor/bhy065.

[58] Robert D. Rogers and Stephen Monsell. "Costs of a predictible switch between simple cognitive tasks." In: *Journal of Experimental Psychology: General* 124.2 (1995), pp. 207–231. ISSN: 0096-3445. DOI: 10.1037/0096-3445.124.2.207.

[59] Jharana Rani Samal, Arun K. Pati, and Anil Kumar. "Experimental test of the quantum no-hiding theorem." In: *Physical review letters* 106.8 (2011), p. 080401. DOI: 10.1103/PhysRevLett.106.080401.

[60] Jesse Schell. *Information Flow: The Secret to Studio Structure: Keynote.* 2015. URL: https://www.youtube.com/watch?v=y92-vkyHKbY.

[61] Claude E. Shannon. "A Mathematical Theory of Communication." In: *The Bell System Technical Journal* 27.July (1948), pp. 379–423.

[62] Claude Elwood Shannon and Warren Weaver. *The mathematical theory of communication.* 10th ed. Urbana: Univ. of Illinois Press, 1964. ISBN: 978-0-252-72548-7. URL: https://www.loc.gov/catdir/enhancements/fy1616/98230924-b.html.

[63] Steven A. Sloman and Philip Fernbach. *The knowledge illusion: Why we never think alone.* New York: Riverhead Books, 2017. ISBN: 9781509811069.

[64] Nassim Nicholas Taleb. *The black swan: The impact of the highly improbable.* New York: Random House, 2007. ISBN: 978-1400063512.

[65] Toyota (GB) PLC. *Muda, Muri, Mura - Toyota Production System guide - Toyota.* 2013. URL: https://blog.toyota.co.uk/muda-muri-mura-toyota-production-system.

[66] G. Trentin. "Conclusive thought on communication flow, knowledge flow and informal learning." In: *Chandos Publishing, Cambridge, UK* (2011). URL: https://www.academia.edu/4765390/Conclusive_thought_on_communication_flow_knowledge_flow_and_informal_learning.

[67] Ellie Violet. "Desire paths: the illicit trails that defy the urban planners." In: *The Guardian* (5.10.2018). URL: http://www.cired.net/publications/workshop2014/papers/CIRED2014WS_0411_final.pdf.

[68] Michael D. Watson. "Information Theory Applied to Decision-Making Structures." In: *Systems engineering in context.* Ed. by James H. Lambert and William T. Scherer. Cham: Springer International Publishing, 2019, pp. 529–541. ISBN: 978-3-030-00113-1. DOI: 10.1007/978-3-030-00114-8{\textunderscore}42.

[69] Gerald M. Weinberg. *Quality software management.* New York and Dorset House Publ., 1992. ISBN: 978-0-932633-22-4.

[70] Geoffrey West. *Scale: The universal laws of life and death in organisms, cities and companies.* Paperback edition. 2018. ISBN: 9781780225593.

[71] John Whitfield. "The sweet smell of the immune system." In: *Nature* (2001). ISSN: 0028-0836. DOI: 10.1038/news010308-10.

[72]   Wikipedia, ed. *OODA loop*. 2020. URL: https://en.wikipedia.org/w/index. php?title=OODA_loop&oldid=945713346.

[73]   Wikipedia, ed. *Volatility, uncertainty, complexity and ambiguity - Wikipedia*. 11.01.2020. URL: https://en.wikipedia.org/w/index.php? oldid=931354554.

[74]   W. K. Wootters and W. H. Zurek. "A single quantum cannot be cloned." In: *Nature* 299.5886 (1982), pp. 802–803. ISSN: 0028-0836. DOI: 10.1038/ 299802a0.

[75]   Shan Xu, Zheng Wang, and Kelsey Woods. "Multitasking and Dual Motivational Systems: A Dynamic Longitudinal Study." In: *Human Communication Research* 45.4 (2019), pp. 371–394. ISSN: 0360-3989. DOI: 10.1093/ hcr/hqz009.

[76]   JAMES WEBB YOUNG. *TECHNIQUE FOR PRODUCING IDEAS*. [Place of publication not identified]: BLURB, 2018. ISBN: 9781388415938.

An Important Final Note

Writers are not performance artists. While there are book signings and public readings, most writers (and readers) follow their passion alone in their homes.

*What applause is for the musician, **reviews** are for the writer.*

Books create a community among readers; you can share your thoughts among all those who will or have read the book.

Leave a thoughtful honest review and help me to create such a community on the platform on which you have acquired this book. *What did you like, what can be improved? To whom would you recommend it?*

Thank you, also in the name of all the other readers who will be able to better decide whether this book is right for them or not! A positive review will increase the reach of the book, a negative review will improve the quality of the next book. I welcome both!